THE FAMILY BUSINESS BOOK

THE

FAMILY BUSINESS

Practical
tips to help
family and
business work
well together

BOOK

PAUL KEOGH

The Family Business Book
ISBN 978-1-912300-58-7
eISBN 978-1-912300-59-4

Published in 2022 by SRA Books
Printed in the UK

All statistics have been sourced through the author's work as the chairman of the National Centre for Family Business at Dublin City University.

Contents

Preface

From Australia to Alaska, from South Africa to South Korea, family businesses are the backbone of all economies globally. Family businesses can be defined differently in terms of ownership or management, but whichever way you define them, according to the National Centre for Family Business at Dublin City University over 75 per cent of all businesses in the world are family owned. Finding reliable statistics on the number of family businesses globally has been a challenge for researchers, policymakers and practitioners. We can only find estimates, even though everyone is in agreement on the importance of family businesses to the global economy. I estimate that there are approximately 24 million family-owned businesses in the United States and some five million family businesses in the UK alone. They range in size from small 'mom-and-pop' stores to some of the largest businesses in the world. Given the size and importance family businesses have to all economies, it is amazing how little tailored support or understanding there is for unique family business issues. I believe this is because policymakers mistakenly confuse family businesses as a generic term for small businesses. Not all family businesses are small or medium. Some of the world's biggest multinationals are family owned: Walmart, Mars and Ford in the US; L'Oréal, Aldi, BMW, Heineken, JCB and IKEA in Europe; and the likes of Samsung in Asia (Asia is the real growth area for family businesses – the National Centre for Family Business reports that at least 85 per cent of China's privately owned enterprises are family owned).

For this book, a definition of a family business is simply 'a business largely controlled by a family'.

Being family owned makes family businesses quite different in a number of ways. For example, they don't have to pander to the stock market like publicly listed companies do. Family businesses often have a long-term perspective where short-term profit isn't the measure of success. They reinvest profits and genuinely want to support and build the communities around where they are based. This means the next generation are key to the ongoing success of family businesses. They will be the value-creators. They understand the modern world and are well placed to embrace technology and adopt best leadership practices. The next generation will be highly educated, well networked and have access to capital. However, there is a major caveat. They may not understand the unique nature and the skills needed to run a successful family business. It is the family issues that could trip them up.

It is difficult enough to have a fully functioning family unit where the family acts *as* a unit and where conflict is dealt with out in the open. Many families are dysfunctional, not necessarily through any fault of their own. No one prepares you to be a member of a family. You don't get to pick your family. You are born into it. We are conditioned not to speak openly about any difficulties we may have within our family unit. In fact, more often than not, we portray a much rosier picture of how a family functions to the outside world. Many family business advisors just take it as gospel that the family functions well as a family and don't interrogate its inner working and the potential for toxic relationships hidden from sight.

Combine the difficulties of running a family and being part of a cohesive family unit with the demands of running a business and you can start to imagine the complexity of such a combination.

There are numerous books on how to run a business successfully. Success in business is down to the quality of your business or service, the niche or business opportunity, your capabilities, being competitive, having good leadership/management personnel and being innovative.

There are many books written on how to run a family business. However, I have always felt that these concentrate on how to run a family business without giving due consideration to issues that arise in the family and the family dynamics, as I will in this book.

Family and business are two worlds connecting and often conflicting.

I have always been interested in family relationships and family dynamics, particularly parent–child and sibling relationships and their ultimate relationship working together in a family business. When a family is in sync and working together within the family business, there is a great sense of belonging and a great sense of 'one big family', including the non-family employees. However, it is hard to imagine a dysfunctional family being able to run a successful family business. Why so many family businesses fail can be down to the number of dysfunctional families outweighing the fully functioning cohesive family units running a business together.

This book is not a psychology or family science textbook. It is intended to be a guidebook for anyone involved in family businesses. Its aim is to stimulate thought on family issues rather than business issues and to give some guidelines on how to approach everyday situations that arise in family businesses from a people perspective.

Introduction

This book takes you through the life cycle of a family business, starting with the founder stage, then through to the crucial stage when family members join the business and on through subsequent generations. Many family businesses don't last past the third generation. Only a small percentage of all family businesses get to the fourth generation and beyond.

In general, success for a family business is determined by issues within the family unit rather than business issues. Key to understanding success and priorities is to ask: **are decisions made on the basis of what is right for the business or are decisions made on what is best for the family?** Sometimes what is right for the business will not be right for the family and vice versa. To understand how and why family businesses survive and thrive we must first look under the bonnet of the family structure.

A family is a form of tribe and tribes survive by utilising their strengths, but they can also perish through rivalries, greed, mistrust and infighting. The concept of family is changing. Families are getting smaller, with parents having fewer children and having them later in life. There is an increase in single-parent families. There are new forms of family units such as same-sex parents and blended families. Divorce is on the increase globally. These changes in family structures will have consequences for the concept of family businesses.

Business is also changing. Technology is replacing many traditional administration and service jobs. New tech businesses are less likely to be family businesses in structure and more akin to colleagues starting a business. These changes are also having a profound effect on family businesses.

This book also looks at family dynamics and some of the issues that arise in families that will ultimately affect the success or otherwise of a family business. Family conflicts are inevitable. How conflict gets resolved is the differentiator and good communication in the family is the key.

Strong families are good communicators. Members of a well-functioning family take the time to understand each other and operate as a unit. This unity is driven by the parents in the first instance. They should know the importance of taking the time to listen, talk and understand each other. Poor communication will make a family dysfunctional, and a dysfunctional family will make a family business a difficult place and could ruin the business. With this in mind, understanding the role of communication is an underlying theme throughout the book.

As the entrepreneur develops the business, the role of the children in the business is a pivotal point for the company and I touch on many of the aspects relating to the next generation, whether they are the second generation or subsequent ones. For example, often family members join a business not having either the right experience or qualifications, which creates tensions within the business. This is why a key aspect of running a family business is to have rules in place, with checks and balances in terms of governance – which includes rules on family members joining the business. Rules also need to be in place for succession planning. It may surprise you to see how few family businesses have a succession plan in place. This aspect proves to be a very difficult area for most family businesses and is often fudged or handled extremely poorly. 'Rags to riches and back to rags by three generations' is often quoted in the context of family businesses but, with the right processes in place and with good communication, it may be avoided.

I discuss the option of selling the family business, an option that is often resisted. This isn't a decision to be taken lightly but I will explore why this might be an option in certain circumstances. Finally, I wrap the journey up by examining the underlying theme – that good communication is fundamental for running a successful family business.

I have worked virtually all my life *inside* family businesses, first as a family member and then as a senior non-family executive in large family businesses on three continents. Families are slow to seek help with family issues and I hope by reading this book that families will realise that conflict is healthy. It is how you deal with it that matters. My observations are from being directly involved with families in business and not from an academic perspective. There is no more complex environment to navigate through than a family business and there is no one model to follow in running a successful one. Successful family units are good at communicating with each other and with non-family people. It is hard to imagine a dysfunctional family running a successful family business.

One aspect of my work that deeply upsets me is when I see a family business conflict destroy the harmony of that family. It is soul destroying to see a family letting a business ruin their lives.

Being part of a family business can also be incredibly rewarding. When the family gel together and the business gels likewise, herein lies the true strength and differentiator of family businesses over non-family ones. Family businesses are resilient. They generally have the vision to sustain the family's involvement across future generations.

Communication is key. There are conversations that happen, conversations that need to happen and conversations that don't happen. I want to help families have meaningful and productive conversations.

I hope that this book helps to stimulate thought and discussion for family members in business together, people that work in family businesses and advisors to family businesses alike.

1

The Entrepreneur-Founder Stage

Looking back, I didn't make life easy for myself. I'd only just got married, was working hard to save a bit of money and decided to start my own business, all within a very short period of time. Before I knew it, I was juggling a young family and a new business. Planning was a bit on the hoof.

Combining family and business is a very complex process. Families are complex in themselves, and no two families are the same. Each one has its own idiosyncrasies shaped by history, personalities, and relationships – family dynamics are a key ingredient in the likely success of a family business. Business is similarly complex and full of challenges – they are different to the complexity and challenges in the family environment. Families need to talk about the implications of being a family running a family business. If it is planned properly, a family business has many advantages over non-family ones. If you get it wrong, a badly structured family business can ruin the family or the business or both.

Founders of businesses spend the first few years of their business life concentrating on establishing and growing the business. They tend to be all-or-nothing people. They have little time for anything else and family life often suffers because of the long hours it takes to get a business off the ground. The personality and way the company is run is often a mirror image of the personality and way the founder operates in life generally; however, family members may join a family business not realising that the business is run as an extension of the personality of the founder. Let's explore this aspect a little.

The importance of the founder's personality

In the entrepreneurial stage, the personality of the owner will dictate how the company is run, its culture, its values and its style of doing business. Many first-time entrepreneurs have little or no experience running a business. The entrepreneur is driven by instinct and gut feeling. They know the market; they saw the gap and they went after it. Founding entrepreneurs often have authoritarian leadership styles – they are used to doing things their way and this can make them difficult to work for. They may have worked in business but running a business for themselves is all consuming. Much if not all of the business plan is inside the head of the founder, and it is difficult for others to know or follow the strategy. Founders can often be secretive and keep their cards close to their chest, not trusting people in general and running their business with a degree of paranoia.

So it is easy to see how a family business often becomes an extension of the founder with their personality and values becoming the brand personality, especially if their name is over the door. If they are creative, they might change their mind frequently and pay little attention to detail. If they are technical, they may find it hard to explain concepts. If they work themselves hard, they might expect everyone else to put in the same hours. Often founders think that a caring, praising and encouraging style of management is a sign of weakness, particularly in traditional industries such as farming or construction. Founders won't have learned leadership skills and they may not have managed people before. They might not even know what emotional intelligence is. Starting a business is hard work and they may not have time to stop and think. Founders are also often inflexible and difficult to work for and, as they transition into a family business, the culture is already set in their image.

Understanding the personality and motivations of the owner of a family business is key to being a successful 'employee' whether as a family member or not. Let's take one example – the founder of the family business who has dyslexia. In this business, the founder might be very bright, intelligent and articulate but will have difficulty reading, writing or spelling. They will be very creative, a good storyteller, good at sales, design, building or engineering. They will have excellent long-term memory for experiences, locations and faces. They can have difficulty using their mobile phone to its full potential. If you don't take the time to understand the personality and traits of such a person, you will not be effective in this family business.

A large cohort of entrepreneurs started out on their own because of being born with dyslexia. This is because their brain is 'wired differently' and working for themselves was a necessity. The school system failed them. They had no choice but to find work rather than go on to further education. Some of the best-known entrepreneurs over the years have had dyslexia. Henry Ford, Sir Richard Branson, Steve Jobs, James Dyson, and thousands of entrepreneurs just like them; all had dyslexia. It is understood that some 35 per cent of start-up entrepreneurs in the US have been found to have dyslexia. I have worked with founders that have dyslexia and their ability to visualise and conceptualise is amazing. They see the world differently and this is why so many are seen as 'geniuses'.

Another reason for focusing on people with dyslexia is not only to highlight how common it is in the business world, but also because these entrepreneurs serve as examples of how business can be approached differently. Richard Branson, like many others with dyslexia, didn't know he was dyslexic and just thought he was stupid in school. He had difficulty writing and spelling. He knew, however, he could retain lots of information and was very inquisitive about things in general. He came to realise he saw the world through different lenses. He surrounds himself with people good at numbers and detail. He doesn't read big reports. He likes information presented visually in graphs or diagrams and the whole Virgin organisation knows that Richard is dyslexic and operates accordingly. He is the creative force, the ideas person.

Anyone that has worked for an entrepreneur who has

dyslexia knows that the company operates differently. Communication adapts. Much of the communication, for example, tends to be verbal as emails may not be read. Visuals and pictures are more common than long written reports. Business owners with dyslexia overcome any problems by finding unique ways to run the business. It's this ability to adapt and communicate ideas that helps them succeed.

> *I am in my fifties and run a very successful family business. I didn't know I had dyslexia until recently. Some people commented on my handwriting but never said anything more. When I was told I was dyslexic I didn't tell anyone. I was uncomfortable. Now it all makes sense. People often refer to me as genius meets madness. I just see the world differently and I see business opportunities. Now that my children have joined the business and one or two, not all, have dyslexia, I have taken a great interest in the whole subject because I found out that 80 per cent of dyslexia is believed to be inherited and this has implications for the next generation.*

Entrepreneurs with dyslexia illustrate the importance of understanding the influence the founder has on the way a business is run. In this case, they often communicate verbally rather than in writing and they can visualise the future more easily than most. They can also be hard to work for because they get frustrated that people cannot see an opportunity as they see it.

> ## TIP
>
> Before you join a family business, either as a family member or an outsider, take the time to understand the founder or the current family business owner, his/her personality, values, style of doing business and the culture created. The ability to communicate effectively and to be effective in a family business depends on your ability to adapt to the environment. Family businesses can be very different environments from non-family businesses. Make sure you are compatible.

When does a business become a family business?

It is difficult to say when exactly a business becomes a family business. It could be one from inception or it could happen without you realising it. Children grow up and suddenly they are spending their school holidays working in the business and then, before you know it, they are fully fledged members of this business. There was no discussion or planning – it just happened. And it isn't just with children this can be an issue; it can happen with spouses too – which can lead to problems in later life!

My partner put some legal forms in front of me, saying that he needed another signatory to get the business started. I signed them but didn't know the consequences. He could have been remortgaging the house. He probably was!

> **TIP**
> A simple rule of thumb is that a business becomes a family business when more than one family member is involved in the ownership or the running of the business.

An entrepreneur can engage with other family members to join him/her in business too and there can be any number of iterations of family members joining together. The entrepreneur probably does not consider this to be a family business at that time. Traditionally, family businesses have started like this in the retail, hospitality and service sectors. Builders, electricians, carpenters and many wet trades can grow from small beginnings as loosely formed family firms to become some of the world's largest privately owned businesses.

My brother and I were very close in school. I was a little older than him. I asked him to join me in a business venture. We didn't really stop to think how the dynamics between us might change. We spent a lot of time talking about our respective roles and how we would work together. This dialogue was essential. We work really well together as a result.

> ## TIP
> **If you are at the early stages of your company's existence, think carefully about becoming a family business in structure and the consequences both good and bad.**

The role of outside advisors

Family businesses have a healthy mistrust of 'outsiders', particularly when it comes to advice on family matters. They tend to try and solve problems within the family, sometimes extending the request for advice to the wider family but seldom outside it. This reticence is regrettable because a well-trained, experienced outsider is one of the most valuable sets of eyes and ears for the family to benefit from.

Running a business and being the boss can be a lonely experience. As the business grew, I knew I would need people to give me honest advice and not be telling me what they felt I wanted to hear. I found a 'consigliere' – an advisor who had years of experience advising family business owners. My consigliere was instrumental in anticipating any potential family conflicts.

A family business needs all the usual array of advisors – tax advice, legal advice and so on – but the family business benefits most from an experienced 'family business practitioner' who has worked with many families that are in business. Doctors run medical practices, lawyers run law practices – they apply and adapt the knowledge they have to help clients. Over the years, I have noticed that successful intergenerational family businesses brought on board family business advisors early in their life cycle.

TIP

The best family advisors have had careers working *inside* family businesses. To have been successful and effective at a senior management level in a family business and not be one of the family is a unique skill. They must be equally skilled at the people/family dimension as they are at the business aspects. It is not easy to find these people, but they are out there. They not only have the theory and the knowledge but they have put it into 'practice' in many family business settings.

2

Family Structure

I have ended up with a very complex family structure. It started as a basic nuclear family – married with children. I had only got my business up and running and divorce struck, then remarriage and stepchildren. I hate to think of how this will all pan out.

'Family business' is two words, but they also represent two different worlds. We need to understand 'families' as well as 'businesses'. Before you can truly understand family businesses, you have to have a basic understanding of families and how they operate.

For example, when a family business is looking for a loan from a bank, the bank asks for the standard business case presentation. They rarely, if ever, ask about the family structure. Quite often, money is lent to family businesses with no questions asked about how the family is constituted and the governance structures in place. Banks, like many institutions, are not comfortable asking questions about the family. Ironically, even though they must do their due diligence, banks feel asking about family is somewhat 'private'. With a better understanding of family matters, better business decisions can be made. After all, in a family business, it would seem obvious that you need to understand family as much as business.

Giving a definition of family is difficult. Does it mean people related by blood and marriage? The family is a system, and its members are all intertwined. When one reacts a certain way, others react accordingly. Every family has relationship challenges: conflict, blame, criticism and rejection. It is complex. There is no such thing as a 'normal' family, but the important consideration is to be a functioning one. Functioning families have learned to live together and thrive.

A hundred years ago, the pace of life was slower; communication was largely face to face and not through a mobile app. People were more local. Grandparents were nearby. Two-parent families were the dominant family structure. Women didn't really work outside the home and the children went to the mother to talk about their emotions, feelings and relationship issues. The father was the breadwinner. He was out working. Families were larger than they are today. Large families learned to live together, and each member took on a role within the family unit often determined by birth order. Families spent a lot of time together.

Today, family life is a lot different. It is much faster. People lead separate lives in separate locations and communicate by way of WhatsApp, Instagram, Facebook or whatever. So, when considering family businesses today, it's important to note that not only are family structures changing but also the way of life. These changes will have a serious impact on the future dominance of family businesses as a business form.

In the developed world, two-parent households are on the decline as divorce, remarriage and cohabitation are on the rise. Families are smaller now. People are having children later in life. There is a drop in fertility and an increase in single-parent households, typically based with the mother. The traditional family structure of a man and a woman marrying and having children is in decline. Same-sex couples having children are on the increase. What constitutes a family is constantly evolving, and blended families – a household with a step-parent, step-siblings or half-siblings – are also on the rise. The extended family – grandparents, married offspring and grandchildren – is still the most common type of family structure in the world, but this nuclear family is no longer the norm. Voluntary childlessness among couples is also common.

Even in India, where it is widely believed that 95 per cent of registered firms are family businesses, there are similar patterns. Fertility rates have fallen, and children are being born later at a time when life expectancy is increasing and couples are separating more, albeit at a much lower rate than in Western societies. Nevertheless, in most Asian countries, including India, there is a growing proportion of divorces with young children. Divorce is as high as 50 per cent in some developed countries. This leads to the concept of binuclear families that have been split by divorce into two separate households, one headed by the mother, and one headed by the father, with the original children from the family residing in each home for periods of time.

Profound changes are happening in China also. In common with the rest of the world, business in China, contrary to perception, is predominantly family owned. Eighty per cent of private enterprises are classed as family businesses, some 20 million of them even though the family concept is more akin to that of an extended family. The Chinese government directly intervened in family structure and caused major household changes. Due to the One-Child Policy, which lasted 35 years until 2016, Chinese family business will face a succession crisis in a few years' time. The vast majority of family firms are still first generation, and the problem is that many of these sole male heirs have no desire to join the family business. They are often extremely wealthy and want to be involved in tech and financial investments. China must face up to significant family business transformation as a result of changes in family structure. Households of three people are now the most common type. Divorce is also on the rise and single-person households are growing rapidly.

The role of women in the family is also changing, in the West and slowly elsewhere. Women have been the traditional caretakers of the family and the majority stayed working in the home. Today, women are better educated and have better opportunities than previously. More women are working outside of the home. There are more women entrepreneurs. Women are increasingly becoming empowered. They are living longer. They are thinking long term and not just about being mothers. There is a greater chance of them being widowed. What impact will this have on family businesses? Increasingly, choosing the family successor is based on merit rather than gender, and women are leading family businesses in greater numbers than ever before.

Family structure changes are making family cohesion more challenging. Families are becoming more racially, ethnically, religiously and politically diverse. This signals the decline of the traditional family as we know it. On a positive note, it will probably allow more women into the workforce and in turn more female entrepreneurs will come to the fore as they shed their traditional role as homemakers. As people are freer to travel and want to travel, globalisation will continue to increase at the rapid pace we are witnessing. In poorer parts of the world, it means that families and family members will move across the globe in search of better conditions.

Meanwhile, people are retiring later and life expectancy is going up, making it possible to work in a family business later in life or for longer.

The world is changing, and all these changes will have a profound effect on the structure of family businesses. The good news is, irrespective of the changes that are occurring in family structures globally, the family is still the universally accepted basic unit of society. A well-functioning family is an asset to society. A dysfunctional family is a burden. This book illustrates how this applies directly to families in business.

TIP

Look carefully at how your family is structured. The leaders in the family setting may not be the right leaders in the family business setting. Do an honest assessment of the strengths and weaknesses of all your family members as members of that group called 'family', including the ones who, at this stage, show no interest in joining the family business. Be realistic: some family members will not be suitable for a role in the family business.

3

Family Dynamics

No two families are the same. We kind of knew raising a family would not be easy. We worked hard at making every member of the family feel valued in their own way, giving them a sense of belonging. Constant communication seemed to have been the key.

The most effective families, no matter how busy they are and how separated they are in geography, still celebrate family occasions, have dinner together, spend time together in activities and use the time they have to get to know each other. They work hard at communication. However, even these families will have conflict and not every family member will get along. After all, we don't get to choose our own family members and sometimes, even after trying very hard, some members of a family may never gel. We must recognise this, especially when we are considering who should join a family business.

The relationship between husband and wife, for example, sets the tone for the family. If the husband

and wife are not getting along this will cause stress for the whole family. This will also cause difficulties when children join the family business, as they will tend to go to the parent who suits their cause.

Sibling rivalry happens in all families. Often this rivalry can be healthy. It can manifest itself in being competitive at sport, for example. Where it is not healthy is when children feel they have to fight for attention or affection. This can lead to jealousy and mistrust in later life. This is something we will revisit later in the book.

In this chapter we explore some of the key family relationships within a family business and some of the issues that can stem from them.

Father and son

The most common family working relationship is that of a father and his son or sons. Traditionally, the business was left to the oldest son to run, and the rest of the family got subordinate roles. In agriculture particularly, farms were handed down from father to son for generations. Respect and self-esteem were measured on a scale of hard work and the hours you worked as the heir apparent.

The patriarchal family structure was the most common structure until recently and it's still the most common in some cultures such as China. Primogeniture, where the eldest child (usually the eldest male) inherits everything, is still common throughout the world and especially in many Asian countries.

An understanding of the relationship between the father and son is crucial in a scenario where they work together. Many fathers and sons get on really well together in both home life and work. When this relationship works, it forms a really effective harmonious operating model. This situation is the exception rather than the rule. The history of family businesses is littered with conflict between the founder and his son(s) in particular, such as Henry Ford and his son Edsel, who frequently disagreed and argued.

> **TIP**
> The greatest threat to family business longevity is not from external sources but from influences within the family. Sometimes fathers and sons are too alike in personality without either admitting it. How far did the apple fall from the tree?

The relationship between the father and his sons can differ depending on where the sons come in the birth order, and with the traditional model where the eldest son either expects to be given the business or is expected to run it, this is often where the tension lies. The other sons are not under the same pressure.

In recent years, fathers have been much more active in helping with the parenting of children from an early age. The increased interaction between fathers and their sons, especially during adolescence, has had a positive influence on the father–son relation. Previously, the eldest son may not have seen much of the father as the latter was busy building up the business. The son had to fight hard for any attention from his father. He might have been upset when the father missed childhood milestones (school plays, football games) due to the pressure of work. By the time the father got home the children were in bed. The son, in this situation, may be longing for the father's approval. The father, on the other hand, sometimes finds it hard to accept that his son has grown up and he still treats him as if he is that boy in short pants. The father is used to being the only boss and it can be difficult changing that mindset.

I built this business from the ground up. I kept my cards close to my chest. I didn't trust anyone. The secret of my success was secrecy itself. I don't know if I can change. I don't know if I want to. When my son joined the business, I had to change. I had to learn to be both a father and a boss. Thirty years later, we are still working at this!

Sometimes the son is in his forties and still has no decision-making authority. The son could be married and have children. He wants to be in charge. His wife is pushing him to take charge and the father is reluctant to relinquish any control. He gives the son some big title to appease him. This doesn't work. The son wants control of the business, but the father is reluctant to retire or may not think that the son is ready to take over the business.

A father should set out clear expectations for his son joining the business before the son joins at all. He should make sure he understands why the son wants to join the business. There can be many reasons, from pride and a desire to carry on the legacy to more self-centred aspirations to be his own boss and not have to work for anyone. Many founders were not wealthy starting off in business. More often than not their children have wealth. They may also have a sense of entitlement. This is not good. It can be surprising to the general public when they read of conflict in family businesses, and the conflict can be vicious and soul destroying. There are countless family business stories that involve a son trying to oust his father from the business and the hatred that ensues. Often this conflict is exacerbated because the son grows into a mini version of the father and they can't see how alike they are. This similarity is often the source of conflict.

What else would I do? I've spent my life building up this business. My name is over the door. I never had time for hobbies. Quite frankly, I've no interest in retirement. The French have a saying: 'Après moi, le deluge'. I am in agreement with this sentiment from Louis XV: I don't really care what happens to the business after I die.

The father might see the son as being ungrateful, unappreciative and in a hurry to get his hands on the business. The son, in turn, may see the modernisation of the business being hampered by the father always doing everything the way he has always done it and surrounding himself with yes men and not really listening to anyone.

The potential for conflict between generations has never been greater. We appear to have lost the art of sitting down and having meaningful conversations. Men are traditionally terrible at this but now, with technology, they can avoid face-to-face communication, leading to confusion and worse conflict. But good communication is the key to a successful father–son relationship and good communication skills can keep both the family and the business working effectively.

Father and daughter

In the old days, daughters were probably left out of any family discussions about the family business. Daughters were helped to prepare for marriage and motherhood, but not business. A daughter may have worked in the family business over the summer, but the father did not contemplate the daughter having a role in the business full time. Nowadays, this is changing. More and more daughters are joining family businesses and, although this is still a relatively new trend, it is in line with the growing number of women in business and management generally.

While fathers and daughters can experience the same issues that affect fathers and sons, they can often have different dynamics too. It can often be less competitive and less confrontational. Fathers seem to accept criticism more readily from daughters. A daughter might feel less of a threat. As time goes by, there can still be tension and conflict when the daughter becomes pregnant and takes time away from the business to be with her children. Again, with good communication before the daughter joins the business, this should be discussed. Many daughters are afraid to mention this for fear of not being given the right opportunity.

The relationship a father/owner has with a daughter can change when she wants to be considered the successor to the business. Fathers can resist this not on merit or ability but being afraid that the daughter cannot raise a family and run a business at the same time. It can be especially difficult for daughters on farms, where they may not be considered as possible successors because the farmer/owner is afraid of a son-in-law getting control of the family farm and changing the name of the farm to his, and the legacy dies. Again, this requires open and honest communication from both parties.

It is difficult for daughters in family businesses, especially if they have brothers in the business too. Some have voluntarily, or not, fallen into the background and taken a lesser role than a brother. If they are to be the chosen ones as successors, they must typically work harder to show their suitability than their male counterparts. They must be more visible to the rest of the staff, customers and stakeholders in order to overcome the 'invisibility' of women in family businesses.

> **TIP**
>
> Daughters must develop a clear strategy on how they are going to take over from their fathers. They need to be seen to be more independent of mind. They should work hard at developing their own profile in the business community, more so than their male counterparts who were probably expected to take over the business anyway. Women commonly network well with women but to succeed as the new 'boss', they must also be good at networking in a male environment.

Wife/mother

Many family businesses start where the wife or partner is the 'copreneur' – both working in the business although often one drops out to rear the children. Don't underestimate the role the mother plays, not just in the family but in the family business also, even though she may not be active in it. The role of women in society is changing rapidly and, in this context, I am referring to the wife of an entrepreneur and mother of their children (it could easily be mother and entrepreneur and stay-at-home dad). Irrespective of this, the children will generally go to the mother to express their feelings. The mother works behind the scenes, listening to the children and their worries. The mother may not necessarily know the ins and outs of the business, but she is driven by a sense of fairness for all her children. Her first priority is the preservation of the family and when there is conflict in the business between the father and the children, the owner's wife takes on the role of mediator in the dispute.

There is also a constant increase in the number of female entrepreneurs. There have only been a few female founders of family businesses hitherto, but the number of female entrepreneurs is growing and with this will come female-led family businesses.

We will see later that female owners of family businesses can have different attitudes to issues such as succession planning and indeed conflict.

An increasing number of marriages are ending in divorce and the lifestyles of founders/entrepreneurs can contribute to the chances of this happening being ever more real. A second wife may not just be marrying into a new family but also into a family business. She can be met by suspicion. It can raise concerns about inheritance, for example, and all this must be resolved by having meaningful conversations among everyone.

Cousins

As the business develops into the second and subsequent generations, the opportunity for cousins to join it becomes a reality. Cousins are much less likely to have an emotional bond to the company – they come from a different part of the family tree. They are a product of in-laws and wider family members. Still, cousins often join the family business without the right scrutiny. Many are not qualified for the job they are given, and cousins (just like in-laws) are very difficult to fire.

I hired a nephew of mine. Didn't think much about the consequences. He turned out to be useless. Every time I tried to get rid of him, my sister would contact me and use emotional blackmail on me, and I'd end up keeping him. In hindsight it was very bad for staff morale.

In-laws

When a family member marries, they begin a journey to build their own family with its own dynamics, its own challenges, its own goals. In-laws can feel like outsiders, especially in a close-knit family. They can feel overwhelmed by the spouse's family. The dinner table in the TV series *Blue Bloods* springs to mind. Similar to the second-time-around partner, the in-law can be met with suspicion and their motives questioned. Over the years there have been cases where next-generation children of wealthy family business owners have had mixed outcomes when it comes to their partners. Throughout the history of family businesses, in-laws have caused problems and disrupted family harmony. Many movie scripts depict a scenario where the boss's daughter gets married and the son-in-law moves into the family business. The rest of the family think of 'gold digging'. This is why pre-nuptial agreements are seen as essential in business families, alongside family charters and shareholder agreements. Many family businesses set out in their 'rule book' the diktat that no in-laws can join the business and this has evolved because of so many horror stories.

There are as many arguments supporting spousal employment as there are against it. If the spouse is highly qualified for the job and has all the skills necessary to carry out the role, then it may be worth the risk. On the other hand, personal relationship issues with other family members are quite common with in-laws, irrespective of whether they work in the business or not. In-laws, even if they do not work in the business, can cause conflict, especially with emotionally charged pillow talk.

My only son married this girl. She showed no interest in the family business before she got married. Maybe she didn't know how profitable it was. Now she drives my son crazy, telling him to get rid of me, telling him to be a man and take charge. Pillow talk is a real pressure.

> **TIP**
> **The subject of in-laws is polarised. Follow even more thoroughly the thought process about allowing in-laws into the business. Don't underestimate the jealousies that can arise in this new dynamic. Draw up specific guidelines for in-laws: employment and compensation policies, written codes of conduct as well as disciplinary and dispute resolution procedures. In many countries, pre-nuptial agreements are legally binding and these are often necessary to protect the business.**

Remember, although we can't choose our family members, we can choose how we respond and interact with them. Success comes from constant communication, being honest and allowing everyone to be heard and understood. It is the sum of the parts that makes families so powerful. Family harmony is the glue that makes families such a dynamic unit in society. Having a properly functioning family is not easy. It will not happen naturally. It must be worked on. Strong bonds make for strong families and cohesive families strengthen families in business together.

4

Family Conflict

Conflict is good. I practice the 'divide and conquer' style of management. I pit them all against each other. It keeps them on their toes and keeps them guessing.

All families will experience conflict, and this is especially true for family businesses. Conflict can be healthy if managed properly. For example, conflict and differences of opinion can lead us to collaborate to solve problems. The successful families and family businesses are the ones who learn how to deal with conflict effectively. In this chapter I look at some of the most common areas of conflict.

There is much to learn from conflicts that have happened in other family businesses, and you can learn as much from failure as success. However, it is not the pleasure gained by reading about others' misfortune that is important (as in the German term *schadenfreude*) but the lessons learned.

Family rows have happened since time began and

can occur for a variety of reasons – childhood animosity, competition, jealousy, love, loyalty, conflict, inequality, loss, lack of trust and money, to name a few. Many family business conflicts are hot-blooded disputes that escalate, eventually involving heavyweight lawyers who often amplify the conflict, while making large sums of money in the process.

In family businesses, conflict can arise in four areas: tasks, relationships, processes and status/money. Many conflicts start through poor communication or lack of it. In many cases bad decisions are made in family businesses out of sentiment and bad judgement, and you don't have to be a scholar of Shakespeare to see real family conflicts – they are all around us. Poor governance and inefficient conflict resolution structure exacerbate the situation, leading to deep-rooted conflicts between family members, and to problems regarding the valuation of the business and, ultimately, power struggles.

However, family conflicts don't always spell disaster. They can be managed, and that is the beauty of family businesses – the harnessing of emotions, passion and pride into positive energy.

Sibling rivalry

Sibling rivalry is one of the most common sources of conflict within a family business. It has happened as far back as Cain and Abel. Sibling rivalry can often be hidden from parents or suppressed.

Sibling positions and the birth order, for example, can have an effect on family members and how they relate to each other. The oldest child initially gets all the attention, and the parents are ultra-cautious. If their firstborn child climbs up on something, they panic. In contrast the youngest could climb trees and not cause a flutter. The oldest child carries a sense of responsibility and is often the sensible one. The youngest might be more carefree, while middle children have some characteristics of the older and the younger siblings.

Sibling relationships can and will, however, change over time. We may have one type of relationship as children, a different relationship as adolescents and different again as adult siblings. In one family, young brothers might get on great together only to be nearly killing each other as they get older, while in another young brothers might have been fighting each other for parental attention only to grow closer to as they get older. Brother–brother rivalry is only matched in intensity by father–son rivalry, with the father often playing one son off the other. Increasingly there can be sibling rivalry among sisters, either sister and sister or a combination of sisters and brothers.

Families experience different highs and lows during the family life cycle and circumstances such as illness, death or divorce may change the relationship siblings have with each other. Jealousy, mistrust or simply a change of personality – these can all impact sibling relationships.

TIP
Invest the time. Families that work well as a unit put in constant effort to understand that all their members are different, have different views, interests, motivations, anxieties and outlooks.

'That's not fair.' This was heard quite a lot when I was growing up. We all said it as children from time to time. Sometimes we didn't even know why we were arguing but we all hated losing. It may have looked like fighting to outsiders but in reality, we all get on very well.

It is important to understand the relationship siblings have with each other as a predictor of how they would interact with each other if they were to join the family business. Individual family members cannot be understood in isolation from one another but rather as part of the family unit. Families are systems of interconnected and interdependent individuals. It is not unreasonable to expect siblings to continue the relationship they have with the other members of the family when they join together in the family business. The oldest can gravitate into a leadership position but sometimes the pressure to do this leads to stress and anxiety.

History is full of famous sibling conflicts. The Ambani brothers, for example, had a very bitter and public feud over control of the Reliance empire after their father died in 2002. This led to the conglomerate being split, with Mukesh Ambani getting the oil and petrochemicals business and Anil getting the power, telecoms and financial services. (This is an unusual example in that it had a happy ending.)

Another famous case of a feuding family was between Adi and Rudolf Dassler, owners of a shoe factory in Germany, and their sister Marie. Marie hated Rudi for not employing her two sons in the family shoe factory, both subsequently getting drafted and killed in the Second World War. Adi and Rudolf also fought each other for control of the business through the war and beyond. They eventually decided to split the business and one created the brand Adidas and the other Puma respectively.

Things, however, got worse with the second generation, when Adi's son Horst was in charge of the Adidas brand. He was a very good entrepreneur but was very ambitious and stepped over the line by making sports clothing which was not allowed in the family agreement, and he got sued by Puma.

Rudi had a poor relationship with his eldest son Armin, and when Rudi became ill, he changed his will to exclude Armin in favour of his younger brother Gerd. Armin had to go legal to wrestle back control of Puma, with Gerd becoming a minority shareholder.

TIP

Understand the relationships each family member has with the others and use role-playing to see how they would work together. If the rivalry is deep, then think twice about them working together.

Parent and offspring

When a child goes into the family business to do some work during the school holidays, it can be a wonderful experience for them. They usually are assigned to a member of staff to give them 'jobs to do'. There is no real pressure on them. It takes the pressure off having to look for a summer job elsewhere. They can come and go. There is some flexibility. Remuneration might be a little vague, but the bonus is they get to spend some quality time with the parent who they might not see too much of during work hours generally. This pleasant experience is not reality, however, and when they get to join the business full time, they can be in for a rude awakening. Again, if the parents talk openly to their children about joining the business and do this in a businesslike way, many of the potential conflicts can be anticipated.

Often, the expectations family members have when joining the business do not materialise. The rest of the staff engage with them differently. They don't make friends at work. They can feel they might have made the wrong decision. They post-rationalise and say they were put under pressure to join the business. They can feel trapped. Job satisfaction is low and often financial rewards are moderate at the start. More often than not, they settle into the business after some time.

> **TIP**
> Set out in your family constitution a rule that all family members must have five years' experience of working in management outside of the business. Don't have them join at director level – allow them to work their way up somewhat.

Father and son(s)

The fundamental psychological conflict between father and son in a family business is rivalry. The father sees the business as an extension of himself and has great difficulty letting anyone near his baby. Non-family employees are not that threatening as the father always keeps in the back of his mind that they can be fired – not so easy with a son. Often, the father accepts the concept of passing the business on to his son but refuses to face up to it. The son is often spoken to as a child – always the immature boy in the father's eyes. The son, often out of impatience and drive, becomes disrespectful of the father's achievements and his perception of his status in society. He would just like his father to step aside. He does not like being dependent on his father for his lifestyle and income. He might get a big title, a big office and a big car but no real power.

The father–son relationship is shaped almost from the birth of the son. At an early age, most sons admire and even hero-worship their fathers. This turns to rebellion as the teenager tries to form their own identity.

For many businessmen, they have been absent for large parts of the son's childhood due to work commitments. The absence of a father from the early years of a child's life leaves a void and can have a negative impact on the son. The son may not be so outgoing and lacks self-confidence and warmth. The son then joins the business and, in this scenario, there wasn't a strong bond there in the first place to build upon.

The father may act irrationally and erratically to the son, often in public. Both the father and son know that this conflict is doing irreparable damage to their relationship and causing many family rows. The father can't see past the son being ungrateful and unappreciative and the son feels both hostile to his father and guilty for being so hostile. The father can't bring himself to believe the son will ever be as good as him at running the business. The son waits for years to take charge.

The son thinks of leaving but is filled with emotions of disloyalty, so he stays. The father loses respect for him for not leaving and trying something on his own. Sometimes the conflict spills over into other family members, particularly the wife of the owner, the mother of the son and often the wife of the son too.

Many father–son conflicts end up in bitter court battles, but many get resolved. Outside advisors play a key role in the father–son relationship's success. They act as very useful mediators. They can work with the son to understand his frustrations and see if any middle ground can be achieved. The son, struggling with his own dependency, is more likely to keep fighting the father rather than to plan to escape his father's control.

It is always terrible to see fathers and sons at war, especially when friends and family can remember them as buddies, heading to sports events and holidays together before they worked together. Is any business worth the alienation of a father and son?

Marriage breakdown

Marriage is probably the most important relationship decision a couple will make in their lives. Married adults now divorce much more often than they did 20 years ago.

Many families have internal conflicts and hide them well from the public eye, but divorce is very public. Divorce can affect every family member and will often spill over into the family business, especially if both parties are shareholders. Divorces can be bitter, and the aggrieved party often wants retribution. With divorce, there is an inevitable split of assets. Some countries have strict rules on pre-nuptial arrangements and in this case, you should think carefully about what you put into the shareholders' agreement and how shares can be transferred (such as a company share buy-back scheme). Even if the spouse is not a shareholder, a family law court might take into consideration the role both spouses had in the running of the business. Different aspects go into the analysis of 'valuable contribution'. The family court could decide that the recipient spouse is entitled to some monies from the company if the company is profitable and has sufficient cash and distributable reserves. In the case of farming, the family home is often on the actual farm itself, making divorce very complicated.

Another aspect of divorce is the effect on children, especially if one or both parents enter into new relationships. Custody battles are not uncommon. Down the road, you are faced with having to make decisions about stepchildren and who should be allowed to work in the family business if you remarry and have another family. All outcomes of divorce will have a bearing on the family business one way or another.

It is interesting to see how many successful family business owners have managed to stay married. Maybe they realise divorce is one of the costliest experiences in their lives and their wealth can be halved overnight.

The breakdown of a marriage is a hugely stressful event and can have significant financial implications for the parties to the marriage and family members. This is particularly the case where the family business is a significant asset where value can be extracted or a notional value can be placed on this to agree funds to be given to the spouse.

TIP

Remember when you are drawing up your family charter to consider the four D's – divorce, death, disability, and debts. Each one of these can have a seriously detrimental effect on a family as a result of having a family business.

Lack of defined roles

One great strength of a family business is the way everyone chips in when there is a crisis, but this is also one of the biggest sources of conflict too – the lack of defined roles. Everyone being involved, day in, day out, can create a very stressful environment. It is not uncommon in family businesses to see little or no formal structures. Often every family member attends every meeting no matter what the subject matter is. Some come well prepared and have researched the subject matter and done their homework and others may simply breeze in. This level of dysfunctionality leads to tension and conflict.

We all chip in. There is no bureaucracy. We don't get bogged down on organisational charts. We roll up our sleeves and get the job done.

In many family businesses, family members are given impressive job titles with little or no job description to support the role, and the vagueness of their role causes them stress. The stress comes from not being sure as to what is expected of them. In circumstances where the roles are not clearly defined, the core principles of business – those of responsibility and accountability – are non-existent. This will often come to light when there is a crisis. Who was responsible for that? Was anyone held accountable?

TIP

Especially with family members, people must have a defined role in the company. The tendency is for them to dip in and out of functions and this causes stress and confusion for the non-family employees. One family member – one very specific job.

Unfair treatment and expectations

Conflict can also arise when one family member perceives that they are being treated unfairly or is actually being treated so. They might have been led to expect or been promised a particular role, or remuneration or whatever, and didn't receive it. Sometimes the family member may have assumed that they were entitled to something and misjudged the situation. Or sometimes one member is seen to 'not be pulling their weight' and getting away with it. Even though families do not admit it, there can be a sense of favouritism where one child gets off lightly. Again, much of this type of conflict is caused by lack of clear communication.

On the topic of fairness, women often think differently to men, and mothers can place great emphasis on 'fairness' and 'equity' when discussing the children, which can have unintended effects. Often the mother would like all the children to have an equal share in the business and equal roles, which is very often is not the right approach for the business, and this can lead to conflict.

> *I want all my children to be treated equally. I don't see why one child should get an opportunity that is not offered to all. If they join the family business, they should join as equals.*

Another tricky situation is when the founder or boss feels let down by the child's ability. This can arise when the entrepreneur/founder realises that his/her children do not have that same entrepreneurial flair that they do. The realisation that entrepreneurs do not breed entrepreneurs can lead to conflict. The next generation will have different skills but may not be entrepreneurs. Acceptance by everyone of this fact can resolve conflict.

Misconduct of a family member can also cause conflict. It can affect the reputation of the company. Substance addiction and other similar matters should be dealt with in the same way as all employees are managed. The family charter should set out the rules for appropriate conduct for family members in the business.

Money

The family's attitude to money can also lead to conflict. When a business is up and running and making good money, the founder, who often was not around to see their children growing up, might throw money at the children by way of guilt. Their relationship to money and their sense of value can then become distorted. For example, sometimes the children might take money for granted and could be summed up in the phrase 'silver spoon'. Money in family businesses can often be the source of much conflict and, if not handled effectively, it can turn into outright war, with the resultant collapse of the business and ruination of the family.

Reducing and resolving conflict

The ability to reduce and resolve conflict depends on your ability to recognise the cause of the conflict and what is causing it. It can be purely family issues or business issues or both.

To be successful at resolving conflict, you have to nip it in the bud early. You must act quickly and decisively. Listen first to what is being said. Pay attention to the emotions and feelings expressed or suppressed. Ask questions to diffuse the situation. If you are perceived to be the cause of the conflict, don't get annoyed and ignore the underlying nature of the conflict.

Decide what the basis for the conflict is – money, greed jealousy, lack of communication, differences in priorities and values, role expectations, respect and recognition, trust issues or simply personality conflict. It could be simply misunderstandings or something deeper.

Once everyone is agreed on the reason for the conflict, try and focus on solving it. Don't get distracted by the tendency to air all grievances that have developed over time. Some past issues may be relevant but don't let the situation descend into an atmosphere of negativity. Keep the conversations civil and calm. Ask family members to speak openly and make sure you have all the facts. Sometimes a family conflict is too deeply rooted and emotional, and it may be advisable to engage a third party to come in and give a neutral balance to the conflict resolution.

TIP

Traditionally, owners of family businesses are not good at conflict resolution within families. Often, difficult decisions relating to the family are avoided or, worse, fudged. Be clear and decisive and communicate properly to all involved.

To the outside world, we all try to project an image of 'one happy family'. We rarely admit to having any family problems. We are taught from a young age, 'Don't air your dirty linen in public.'

Conflicts in families and in business inevitably become greater in times of stress. Conflict is hard to resolve because the distrust caused can be deep rooted. Stop believing your outer image of 'one happy family' if it is not true. The more you say it, the more you believe it. Be realistic and honest and you still can function effectively as a family. Recreate meaningful interaction, rekindle family affection, have clear communication and find ways of reducing irrationality and heightened emotions. Conflict is inevitable, but if it is not handled properly, the family will become dysfunctional. As I've suggested before, dysfunctional families generally run dysfunctional family businesses.

5

Governance & Ownership

There's lots of talk about corporate governance. Didn't give this much thought until we became a second-generation business. Delighted that we did put in rules to help the family as well as the controls in the business. Didn't like the idea of a board of directors at first. Felt I might lose control, but the board is a great help to me now.

A family business may have had humble origins and they may have been fairly informal. You may have been a sole trader where you own everything, as well as carrying any risks personally. That is why, as the business grows, most family businesses become limited companies. Like any other limited company, this means that there need to be rules in place as to how the business is run (i.e. governance). It isn't the most exciting aspect of running a business, but it will help ensure its smooth running and shouldn't be overlooked.

Family business governance clarifies relationships, rights and responsibilities, to ensure that the business is managed professionally and responsibly.

Many founders of businesses give very little thought to the structure of their business at the start. A solicitor is engaged to set up the company and often takes boilerplate documents for the memorandum and articles of association. Ask a business owner, a few years later, what these documents specify and many cannot remember. Many business owners have their spouse as the other director and possibly a shareholder. This is the quickest approach, although the solicitor hardly ever warns that there might be consequences if you end up divorced!

Family governance recognises the complexity of family relationships. These can be loving but can also result in nepotism, rivalries and power dynamics. Proper governance enables family business owners to manage both their family business assets and its relationship with the family. It provides structures and processes to manage competing demands and interests of the key stakeholders in the business, and sets rules on how to manage that relationship between the business and the family. Family issues tend to have greater impact as the business moves through the generations. More family often means more issues.

It is amazing how difficult it is to draw an organisational chart for many family businesses. The informality and fluid structure can be both a strength and weakness of a family business. Informal structures are valuable so long as they are understood and act consistently. As the company grows, more formal structures will help, especially in terms of facing a crisis, thus avoiding people making quick decisions without structure, responsibility or accountability.

Ownership

When the business starts, ownership is not an issue as the founder generally owns all the shares. It is only when the company develops and grows that ownership becomes an issue. Some owners start distributing ownership too early to children, before the children have any sense of value. Some owners, fearing family conflict, hold on to ownership, sometimes until they die.

Ownership and the management of the business can often become connected, but ownership is a separate issue from family members running and working in the business. Distribution of ownership from the first generation to the second can often be the most problematic. In general, there are more second-generation family members and hence the shareholder numbers can increase. This can continue into the subsequent generation. In one case, a famous brand has more than 400 family member shareholders.

The distribution of ownership can lead to deep-rooted conflict among family members and their partners. Conflict is inevitable but it is how you handle it that is the key to successful transition.

Having a shareholder agreement in place that attempts to cover all future inevitabilities is essential.

> ## TIP
> Don't be too eager to give shares to your children. Don't confuse 'looking after them financially' with giving them ownership of the company. Explore all other ways of giving them financial security, such as trust funds. The decision to give a family member some ownership of the company should be based on what is best for the stewardship of the company in the future.

Shareholders' agreement and company constitution

A shareholders' agreement is a written contract entered into by shareholders of the company. It is a private document that is not disclosed publicly. Draw up a shareholders' agreement from the start – this will set out the ownership of shares and the rights attached to these shares. It should specify the rules attached to the sale and transfer of shares, including pre-emption rights.

Many disputes in family businesses centre around the value of individuals' shareholding and the definition of 'market value'. It is important to outline how the value is to be calculated. There need to be rules around resolving disputes. The agreement will outline the dividend and borrowing policies. The shareholder agreement should also deal with the disposal of the business, the acquisition of other businesses or any material changes to the business. It should deal with the possibility of the death of a shareholder or permanent incapacity.

The constitution is the governing document of the company and is open to inspection by the public. It will outline the share capital, the classes of shares and the rights attached to the different classes of shares, details on directors' meetings and so on. Because it is a public document, it is written accordingly. The predominant reason for using a shareholders' agreement as well is that it is a private document and can include confidential rules for shareholders. Care needs to be taken to ensure that the constitution of the company and the shareholders' agreement are consistent and do not have any conflicting clauses.

Shareholder agreements drawn up by two shareholders having a 50:50 split should make sure that they include clauses that deal with differences of opinion and disputes. Otherwise, there will be stalemate and disputes will end up in court.

As a family business grows, it starts to consider more the importance of the board of directors. Most shareholder agreements provide that the company is controlled by its board of directors on behalf of the shareholders. The shareholder agreement will specify the structure of the board and who has a right to a seat. It will also cover a provision (or not) for the appointment of outside directors and will specify rules around who is to chair the board. Rules will be included for the calling of urgent board meetings.

Family members as shareholders

Ownership of a family business is often mixed up with running a family business. Family members can own shares in the business and not work in it. Alternatively, they can work in the business and have no ownership.

Decisions regarding family members working in a business are not as problematic as giving away ownership of a business. If a family member is not pulling their weight, you can always fire them! If you give them shares, it is much more difficult to get shares back off them if you are not happy with them.

TIP

Think carefully about granting shares in your business. This decision or the lack of a decision is the main cause for strife in families. It involves money and wealth. It involves power and influence. I have seen family owners give away shares to family members believing it is the right thing to do, only for it to come back and haunt them.

A well-established family business owner warned me not to part with shares until I had to. I didn't listen and gave all my children equal shares. Worse still, I did it to save tax!

I mentioned earlier the notion of 'fairness' when it comes to children. Time and time again, I am in conversations with families and often it is the mother saying she wants 'fairness'. Giving children shares equally may not be the fairest course of action. This sounds counterintuitive.

Dividing anything among people that might have different aspirations, motivations and needs is always fraught with danger and can lead to trouble down the road. There is always a dilemma in discussing the concept of fairness among children of a family business. Fairness is often only seen through your own eyes. You must explain what the rationale is for a course of action; then people can decide whether it is fair and for whom it is fair – whether them, the business or the rest of the employees.

When everything is discussed, debated and agreed, there is nothing more satisfying than to see a family working together and enjoying the experience. The next generation need to be motivated and mentored, and their energy and enthusiasm must be harnessed. Everyone must know and understand the plan, with everyone pulling in the right direction and everyone clear about their roles in the plan.

I work in the business full time. It is not fair that my brother gets shares in the business, and he doesn't work in the business.

It must be explained to family members the difference between ownership and working in the family business. All family members could have a stake in the company and therefore be shareholders. The family members who work in the business are employees. As employees they are paid a salary as employees for the work they do, and they might get a bonus as a result of good performance. They may also own shares. They therefore wear two hats – executives in the company and shareholders in it.

As I said earlier, don't be in any rush to gift shares to your children. If you are in your sixties you are bound to get a call from your tax advisor telling you that you must transfer shares urgently to avoid paying a big tax bill. I have seen owners rushing off to save tax and transferring ownership to their children just in time to beat a tax deadline. It isn't always the best move in the long term.

TIP

You should be thinking about the next generation long before you are staring at a potential tax bill. Don't get me wrong: no one likes paying more tax than they can legitimately avoid. However, I have seen rushed tax measures nearly ruin family businesses if the objectives are not clearly communicated.

Governance structure

At some point all family businesses come to the stage where they ask whether they should include non-family people as directors. Too often, family businesses maintain an informal, 'family only' board long after the business needs have outgrown this structure.

In Latin America, for example, the vast majority of

companies are family controlled with boards consisting of only family members. However, in the rest of the world, non-family directors are becoming more commonplace. External directors are useful for contacts in business, their experience and for making decisions without being emotionally attached to the family. In the early stages of a family business, most operate without a board of directors.

Advisory board

As the business grows and becomes more complex, a first step could be to set up an advisory board. An advisory board is not a legal structure, and the advisors are not directors. They do not carry out any fiduciary duties. Some family businesses prefer advisory boards because the members do not have to be publicly declared. You can have some very senior businesspeople agreeing to be advisors rather than board members because of the confidentiality of it. Advisory board members would ideally be retired senior executives in your industry. If they have been involved with a family business, all the better. They should bring a perspective to the board gained from years of experience. This will balance the family experience, which is probably restricted to their own business. The advisory board candidate should be a senior executive who has wide experience and better to be a generalist rather than a specialist. Someone like this will be extremely valuable to a family business. Besides their role as advisor, they will act as a mentor and often spot a potential family conflict and defuse it before it is allowed to fester.

Board of directors

As the company grows in size and complexity, the family business should move from having an advisory board to a board of directors. It will be used to receiving outside advice but not the governance formality of board meetings and the formal process of decision-making. The board of directors is a more formal structure than an advisory board. The advisory board forms a valuable part of the process of transition from where the owner makes all the decisions towards a more professional structure, providing an intermediate step along the way to a board of directors with independent non-executive professionals.

Ideally the board should be chaired by a non-family director and should have at least two non-family members on it. In the family charter it will specify how many family members sit on the board and the criteria for picking them.

The role of independent directors is valuable to a family business. They can bring an impartial view to the board. They can bring experience and expertise and they can prevent family rows from going out of control. A board consisting only of family members can be very emotional and hard to manage. Good governance suggests that the chair of the board should also not be the chief executive. Many founders of family businesses want to be both. Ideally, if one of these positions is filled by a family member, the other should be filled from outside. Non-executive directors have fiduciary duties and must act in the best interests of the company. A mistake that is often made in setting up a board of directors is to invite friends of the family to join the board. In this case the friend of the family might not want to 'upset' the family and may not be an effective director as a result.

TIP
The board composition should be thought through carefully to maximise its value to the company. Give senior family members professional training as board members and how to maximise the effectiveness of their board.

The ultimate aim of the board is to preserve the strengths of the family-owned company and to identify areas of weakness and advise accordingly.

The board of directors or advisory board should meet at least five times annually, probably the ideal number being eight meetings in a given year. One of the most valuable roles a board will carry out in a family business is the evaluation of the CEO, the senior management and whether family members are the best candidates for senior roles. The board must point out when family members are not up to the roles given them or in positions where they are not capable. The board should also be active in succession planning and help to develop a training plan for the successors and other family members. Sometimes this means going outside of the family to find the right leader and this decision can be very difficult for an all-family board.

The family council

As the family grows in number in tandem with the business growing, you will have family members with differing roles all interested in what is happening in the family business. Some family members are shareholders and nothing else. Some family members might be shareholders and directors. Some might be simply employees and others might be neither owners nor employees.

A family council is a communication vehicle for all family members. It is a family forum separate from the business. It deals with family issues as they relate to being part of a family that owns a business.

In the founder stage, where there are few family members involved, the family council is of lesser importance but as time goes by and the company moves into the second and third generations, the number of family members increases. A family council is most relevant when family members hit a critical size; 20 members is probably a good starting level. As the family grows there will be a need to elect members to the council so that the numbers don't get unmanageable. Whoever is elected chair of the family council may be given a seat on the board of the company, representing all the family interests.

The family council is a structure that gives every family member a sense of belonging to the business, and for the business to keep the family informed. It is the primary link between the family, shareholders, the board and family members.

The family council's core function is to agree what the key family values are that should be vested into the running of the family business and the family's vision for the business. The family council might not have been set up before the family constitution was written but they have the responsibility for reviewing and amending the family constitution/charter when and where amendments need to be made. In this forum, the family get to talk about what matters to them as a family and their roles in the business. It facilitates discussion on a range of matters such as entry into the business, wealth created by the business for the family and the leadership of the business.

Ultimately, the family council sets policies for the family, whereas the board of directors sets policies for the business.

The family council might also have a family office that manages family assets separate from the business. It may also be involved in any philanthropic activity, especially if the family sets up a charity foundation.

The family constitution

Many family business books suggest that a family business generates a document called a family charter, constitution or protocol. These names are not very user friendly, but the concept is valuable. Many families in business find the process of drawing up a family constitution very difficult. They accept the principle that a document that provides clarity on a number of family issues is a good thing, but struggle with pulling the family together in order to pull the document together.

More and more next-generation family members have strong views about the environment and sustainability.

They want these reflected in the way the family business conducts itself. Without a family constitution, these ideological aspirations have no platform. The process of drawing up the family constitution or charter provides a useful forum for family members to air and discuss issues that they consider important to the business and have them reflected in the business. The family constitution lays out a clear vision, purpose and values for the company and defines the role of family members in achieving this vision, whether as shareholders not working in the business, shareholders working in it or simply as family members with no stake in the business at all.

The problem with the family charter or constitution is that everyone will agree that it is a good idea, but it quickly falls into the category of 'nice to have but not immediately necessary'.

Family meetings

Family meetings allow the family to meet and discuss the family business in a slightly formal setting. For these meetings to work, there needs to be clarity of purpose, roles and decision-making. It may or may not include all family members, whether they work in the business or not.

These family meetings can develop into family councils when the family grows and becomes more complex. Take, for example, El Corte Inglés. This department store group began as a small tailor's shop founded in Madrid in 1890. In 1935, Ramón Areces Rodríguez, helped by his uncle César Rodríguez González as partner and chairman, bought out the tailor. By the 1960s, the business began expanding all over Spain and this expansion lasted until the mid-1990s.

During this time, Ramón had been preparing his nephew Isidoro Álvarez to be his successor. Ramón had been managing director since 1966 and knew the business well. In the period from his death in July 1989 to Isidoro's death in September 2014, the company was very successful with strong growth, business expansion and key achievements such as the acquisition of Galerías Preciados and Marks & Spencer in Spain. Two days after his death, the board appointed Dimas Gimeno, Isidoro Alvarez' nephew, as chairman. In 2019, the daughter of Isidoro Alvarez, Marta Alvarez, became chairperson, moving the company into its fourth generation as a family business.

To an outsider, it was a highly successful business but underneath there were serious family governance issues.

Governance issues relating to ownership

Many family disputes relate to the ownership structure of the company. When the business is 100 per cent owned by the founder, ownership isn't a problem. Problems begin to arise when family members join the business. There is often a vague discussion about future ownership but nothing is agreed and put in writing. Time passes and uncertainty looms regarding future ownership. This leads to tension and high emotions.

There should be a shareholder's agreement in place from the point where the shareholder base is opened up that covers all the eventualities of future ownership.

One of the most common governance issues relates to share valuations where family members want to sell their shares. In this case, the shareholders' agreement allowed for the sale of the shares to other family members at a price agreed by the firm. The Areces siblings (César, Ramón, Maria Jesús and Maria del Rosario) decided to break with tradition, and seek 'market value' for the shares, even though two of them worked for the business. The company estimated the shares were worth €35m. The siblings disagreed. The rebellion required the courts of Spain to decide the value of the shares and to free them for individual sale, even though the siblings had no intention of selling the shares at the time. A judge 'resolved' the problem in 2007 and decided the shares were worth €98.52m. El Corte Inglés decided to appeal the decision to the national high court and the media had a field day. Madrid's provincial court upheld the appeal. Meanwhile, the sibling César filed a further appeal to the supreme court. This court ruled that 'the company cannot be ordered to purchase the shares from the shareholding plaintiff for the real value set by the report provided'.

This family dispute cost all concerned millions in legal fees and, in the end, there was an out-of-court settlement nearer the value offered by the company in the first place.

There were other high-profile share valuation disputes that led to deep-rooted bitterness among family members. The company was now in its fourth generation with a large and diverse family ownership. Part of the solution was to appoint non-family directors to the board, experienced businesspeople with good professional backgrounds. Further development has been the appointment of significant non-family senior management to help run what is now one of Spain's largest companies.

El Corte Inglés could not have been expected to see into the future when it set up this family business in 1935. On the 'business' side, the company is a great success. It has the usual business issues – such as the impact of the coronavirus pandemic on retailers and the rise of online sales – but it remains one of the largest department store groups in Europe, employing around 88,000 people.

On the 'family' side, lack of clearly defined family rules and governance led to a wide diversity of owners, which increased the risk of conflict. As the business grew, structures should have been put in place on the family side. The shareholder war could have been avoided if a formal detailed constitution had been in place. It took until the fourth generation to have a fully functioning board of directors with a mix of family and non-family directors. The disputes did significant reputational damage to the company, but the strength of family businesses is that they will learn from this and grow even stronger once the family structures are in place.

6

Succession Planning

I instinctively do all the business planning without hesitation but when it comes to developing a clear plan for the family in the business and a succession plan, I keep finding reasons not to bottom this out.

Chief executives in public companies typically have a tenure of about five to seven years. The planning process to appoint a new CEO is very well organised and is a task given priority by the board of directors. By contrast, chief executives in family businesses often stay in position for longer than 20 years and there is no planned approach to picking the person to take over.

The elephant in the room

The lack of succession planning is the number one elephant in the room when it comes to family businesses. You would be surprised at the number of times a leader of a family business dies without having a plan for his/her replacement. Worse still, dying without a will in place causes havoc both to the business and to the family. I always ask owners the question, 'If you were hit by a bus and killed tomorrow – what is the plan for the business?' Most answer, 'I'm not planning to be hit by a bus!'

Deciding on who is to replace you is probably the most important task you have as a business owner, and it is the one most people procrastinate about. The lack of succession planning in family businesses causes all sorts of problems and ultimately leads many first-generation family businesses to fail.

Two very important aspects get rolled into one and the process gets complicated: who will own the business and who is to run the business. These are two very different things.

A key question that needs to be asked but is very often avoided is 'Should we keep the business in the family?' – i.e. the thought process around keeping the business or selling it.

Likewise, 'Should we continue to have a family member running the business?' – i.e. having a family member running the business or getting someone outside the family to run it.

Often, through lack of clarity in succession planning, the current family member running the business thinks it's a great idea to keep everyone guessing, create competition between siblings and let the strongest survive. In reality, this destroys teamwork and cohesion, creates factions in the company and generally is totally counterproductive.

Bias

Traditionally, family business succession planning has had certain built-in bias. Either the business is deemed to pass from father to oldest son or father to son, but not to daughters.

> **TIP**
> In this era of family businesses, it is best leaving gender aside and assessing your children on their abilities and suitability to the job on hand.

The Torres wine family is an interesting case study of the role of female members in succession. The roots of the Torres family can be traced back to the 17th century, but it was in 1870 that Jaime and his brother Miguel started Torres y Compania. Torres is now the largest winery in Spain, with brands such as Viña Sol, Sangre de Toro, Coronas and Viña Esmeralda. Like so many, it is family owned. They are founding members of Primum Familiae Vini, an association of family-owned wineries.

Torres celebrated its 150th anniversary in 2020 and is managed by the fourth generation – Miguel A. Torres took over after the death of his father Miguel Torres in 1991. Miguel A. Torres knew he was destined to take over the business as that was the rule- – it would move down from father to son. However, Miguel Torres senior had little interest in retiring and refused to pass control to his son. He prided himself on telling everyone he would die while working – a common problem in succession planning. Miguel A. finally had enough of the autocratic style of his father and at the age of 40 he took a year off in Montpellier to distance himself and give the father time to think. Miguel A. then came back into the business, and he started to get more say. His father died and, keeping with tradition, Miguel A. took over as president.

His sister Marimar knew she was never going to be given the chance to run the business. So in 1975, she moved to California and continued as Torres' export director based there. Marimar is fluent in six languages. During the next ten years, she increased the shipments of Torres wines to the US from 15,000 cases to 150,000. Knowing she was never going to be the chosen successor, she built up her own very successful wine business – Marimar Estate vineyards and winery in California.

Cristina Torres, Marimar's daughter, is a member of the fifth generation of the Torres winemaking family. She joined Marimar Estate as director of sales and marketing in 2020.

This is noteworthy because, in the Torres winemaking family, the business has been handed down from father to son for five generations; when Cristina takes over Marimar Estate, this will be the first time in the family history of passing a business to a female.

Miguel A. Torres has a dilemma on his hands. Of his three children, two are in the business – a son and a daughter. Will he keep with the family tradition and appoint his son, even though he has a very talented daughter, Mireia, in the business? Would he be considering joint presidents? In 2012, he seemed to be signalling that his son Miguel Torres Maczassek was the heir apparent when he appointed him managing director of the Torres Group. In 2015, Mireia was appointed head of R&D and innovation at Familia Torres. What is Miguel A. Torres going to do in his succession planning? Maybe Mireia might follow her aunt Marimar's example and set up her own winery. Let's watch this space. Some difficult conversations to be had, I'm sure.

Difficult conversations

It is often assumed that the business will automatically pass to someone in the family, most usually the children. However, it is very important for the family to really interrogate this and ask the questions, 'Why do you want to join the business?' and 'Do you have the skills necessary to run the business?'

Equally important and becoming a more frequent situation is to ask the question, 'Why do you *not* want to join the business?'

Although business owners will often say that they don't talk business at home, something is being communicated. Entrepreneurs work seven days a week, especially at the start of a new business. They take work calls at home, in the car, while watching the kids' football games, wherever. Even if very young, the children cannot but be involved mentally in some way. By a type of osmosis, the children absorb basic knowledge of the business. This is particularly true of farm families, for example. The children love being around the farm and the animals. They grow up spending their youth on the farm and, without any formal learning, they know more about farming than their townie friends.

It is very seldom, however, that a conversation actually takes place between parent(s) and their young children about the children's role in the future of the business. How often have we heard phrases like these:

I was too busy trying to get the business up and running. I never gave any thought to being a family business. The children were only babies, really.

I don't want to put any pressure on my children to join the business.

All my children are welcome to join the business but I'm OK if they don't.

This is often code for not knowing what to do when it comes to the children growing up. As children get older, conversations can be difficult. Sometimes children may work in the business for the school holidays, but this is often done on an ad hoc basis. Many of us have worked in family businesses where the children come in for the holidays, but the owner is too busy or too awkward to mentor them. It is left to the poor unfortunate in that department to think of something to give 'Little Johnny' to do and it makes for a long summer!

Communicating with children, young and old, is easier said than done. It takes time and effort. Parents must know what is going on in their children's lives, understand their beliefs, understand their views and be there to help and guide them. Children should feel comfortable talking to their parents.

This gets difficult, especially when children become teenagers and are conditioned to seek independence, to explore, to seek out relationships outside of the family. It can be a confusing time with hormonal changes. Teenagers learn to 'comply' somewhat because ultimately the breadwinner is their ATM. Even though they are conversing with us to get money, we learn to use this opportunity to chat to them.

Often the problem is that the business is still not considered a 'family business' in the mind of the founder. It can be in existence for many years before the founder starts to consider that the business may be becoming a family business, or sometimes they never think about it. More often than not, the children simply drift into the business. This is generally a recipe for disaster.

Many family conflicts have started as a result of either the children feeling obliged to join the family business or them wanting to join the family business but having little to offer. Don't leave all this unspoken. Don't rely on assumptions and presumptions. Discuss everyone's expectations and motivations openly and do this as a full family.

TIP

It is never too early to think about the next generation and whether there is a role for them in the business. Get to know your children, their strengths and their weaknesses. You may feel you don't have the time, but it is actually time well invested.

Doing nothing isn't an option

Succession planning is a complex process. It takes time and there are many aspects to consider. It shouldn't be rushed but this is no excuse for putting it on the long finger. A founder of a family business has invested as much emotionally as they have financially. They don't want to give it up or pass it on and some prefer to die first if they can't face the task of being replaced. The strategy of doing nothing about succession planning is the most common in reality. People are living longer so it is not unusual to see owners of family businesses still in charge until well into their eighties. This means that the next generation is probably in their fifties before taking over.

My father keeps telling me that I'm useless and if I was in charge, the business would collapse. Then I find out he has transferred the business to me without telling me – when I asked him, he told me that nothing has changed, that he is still running the company.

I don't intend going through the tax considerations and motivations for transferring a family business. My concern is always that in the desire to save tax that you don't end up ruining your business because you were either not prepared for the consequences or you didn't communicate the outcomes properly to family members or, worse, you created a rift because the smell of money set some family members off in a hissy fit.

Here is a reminder of some of the areas to consider in succession planning:

- ↳ capital gains tax
- ↳ capital acquisition tax
- ↳ retirement relief
- ↳ business relief/entrepreneurial relief
- ↳ agricultural relief/business property relief
- ↳ same event relief
- ↳ stamp duty

and so on.

It is easy to imagine that a tax official never ran a family business! Hopefully, someone somewhere in tax policy comes from a family business background and can see how unnecessarily complex this whole area has become.

Check your will

It is surprising how many family business owners have no will made at all or the will was drawn up as a standard domestic will, basically leaving all assets to their spouse upon death. Without a will, your assets will be divided according to the rules of intestacy and may pass to those who you never intended to inherit your assets.

> **TIP**
>
> Dying prematurely without a will made or with an inadequately drafted will is a nightmare for those loved ones left behind. Your family circumstances are complex – you could be single, married, separated, divorced, have children from one or more relationships, have stepchildren, and so on. A will forces you to think about how you want to provide for all or protect some from others.

Options in succession planning

Some business owners do a halfway version of succession planning. They concede to pressure to step down and hand over the reins while moving upstairs to the role of chairperson – and in many cases continue to run the business, just with a new title. Others, however, are quite happy to hand over the reins; they have extensive interests outside of the business and have accumulated some wealth. Some in this group even relish the challenge of starting again with something new – a type of semi-retirement.

There is also a halfway house that is positive. The owner hands over the reins completely in terms of the day-to-day running of the business but is around when asked to be an ambassador for the company. The successor knows the value of having the predecessor on call. Proper rules of engagement are in place and it augers well for continuity.

We saw earlier that there can be many tensions between a parent and child, particularly between a father and son in business together. One is the father's lack of communication regarding his intentions. Retirement is seldom discussed. The next generation get frustrated. They want to try new things. They want to move the company forward, but they can't.

From watching television soap operas about family businesses, we often get the impression that the patriarch somehow, without warning, calls all the family together and announces the new leader. I'm sure this has happened, but it would spell disaster.

Drawing up a succession plan

Drawing up a succession plan is a complex process. It can take up to five years of planning. There are three aspects to it. First, there is a complete analysis of the business to be done – where is it now, where does it want to get to and how will it get there? Second, there is a complete analysis of the people involved in the business, both family and non-family senior management. Third, there is the financial, tax and legal side of any potential decision to be considered.

In the case of larger family businesses, the board of directors is heavily involved in this process, but many family businesses are not structured in such a way and must rely on outside family business advisors to help with the process of succession planning.

In an ideal world, a family business should make an initial decision that they are going to recruit the best person for the job, irrespective of whether they are family or not. In reality, many family businesses make a decision that the successor must be family and if the family member chosen hasn't all the right attributes, they will be trained, developed and supported by senior management to succeed. It is rare that a family business chooses a non-family member to succeed, especially if it is transitioning from first to second generation. It becomes more common in future generations where the business has grown and it is more complex.

The future generations of families throughout the world will be better educated and have more opportunities to travel outside their own geographic area. They will want to travel and see the world. It is not as automatic as it used to be that the next generation will want to join the family business. Also, some family members are happy to work in the business but don't want to lead it.

I work in the family business because it is handy. I get to work around my lifestyle and can go off and do my own thing without having to answer to anyone. I take a lot of time off in the summer. Don't get me wrong – I'm there for all the big decisions.

The choice of who is next to lead the business will have a profound effect on the performance of the family business. A poor leader will lose the company money and probably kill it. A good leader can keep a company going and make reasonable profits for the company. Research has shown that an exceptionally talented leader can more than double the profits generated even by good leaders.

Leadership in non-family businesses requires thousands of hours of preparation, training and experience. People are given many different roles in many different areas on their path to senior management. Competition can be fierce, and they learn to handle all the politics that goes with that. If managers aspiring to be promoted don't get promoted at the pace at which they want it, they leave and join a competitor or change industry or even country. Nowadays, a senior manager might have changed jobs five or six times before they hit their forties. The days of a job for life are gone and people's loyalty to companies is diminishing.

Family members stay loyal to their family business and so too do their employees. This is both a good thing and a bad thing. The family can feel loyal to staff, but the staff may not have been trained and developed and cannot leave because they are not good enough to get another job. This can also be true of family members.

More and more family businesses are recognising the fact that it is important to allow family members to get relevant business experience outside of the business. Parents have given their children the opportunity to get a good education. They also need them to get business experience away from the family business.

In working with family businesses, many next-generation family members feel that they were not allowed to get the relevant experience outside of the company. Others feel that, with hindsight, they rushed into joining the business and didn't have enough general business experience.

Picking one of your own

Picking one of your children to do anything is fraught with problems. If it is something they all want to do, you will be accused of favouritism. If it is something no one wants to do, you will be accused of picking on them.

In an ideal world, we should be assessing our children and their potential to join the family business in terms of their strengths and weaknesses from an early age, definitely no later than their teens.

TIP

Assessing your children's potential for taking over the family business is hard to do. If the children are aware you are doing this, it will put them under undue pressure to join the business. It has to be handled delicately.

If I talk to a young teenager, I have no idea – and probably nor do they – what they are good at. You can see some indicators. Maybe they are full of energy, maybe they are lazy, but all this can change as they get older. Maybe they are very academic but not streetwise. Maybe they are not very academic but have the smarts. Ideally you have one child who is decisive, has a sense of urgency and has quick reaction times. The bad news for family businesses is that the leader must also have empathy and an emotional connection with the wider family. He or she must be able to run the business but not at the expense of family unity.

School reports are a good starting point. Compared to years ago, these give a more rounded assessment of your child's abilities both in terms of emotional intelligence and pure academics.

I founded this business. Had no training whatsoever. I learned everything the hard way. I'm just going to throw my kids in the deep end and may the fittest survive!

In reality, if a family business is to grow and prosper, the parent or leader must grow the business with a combination of skills needed to maintain family harmony, as well as being cognisant of having to prepare the business for life after them.

A realistic talent assessment of your children is a key stage in deciding whether to let them join the business in the first place, let alone thinking of them as future leaders. All parents think their children are great, so you might need an independent assessor to help you take the rose-tinted glasses off! If the only reason a person joined the business was because of their blood, then this is not good for anyone and not good for the business.

Lastly, write down the succession plan. It should include the research and analysis that went into making the decisions. It should outline the stages envisaged and the timescale involved. It should outline the training, development and mentoring programmes to be put in place for the successor. It should outline the senior management team that is best suited to support the successor. The succession plan also needs to be communicated carefully to everyone – the family, employees and stakeholders, such as customers, suppliers, banks and investors. This will help to ensure a smooth transition.

Conclusion

Choosing a successor is not a task family businesses do well. The current boss can favour a family member they get on best with or someone they feel is nearest to them in image and likeness – that may not always be the best choice. The best choice for the business may actually be looking externally for a new leader. A realistic talent assessment of your children is vital but also very difficult. It may hurt people's feelings but you need to do what's right for your situation. When you have chosen your plan of action, write it down and communicate it to avoid unnecessary delay or confusion when you might not be around to resolve conflicts!

7

The Next Generation

I joined the family business without giving it much thought. I believed it was my destiny. I didn't know what I was good at. The pressure of having that well-known surname was immense. I felt everyone was waiting for me to fail. Luckily, my parents had put in place a plan to help me learn the business. I didn't start at the top with a fancy title like some of my friends. I started in sales, learned the product, sold a lot of it and advanced that way. When I took over the business, I was ready, and I had proven myself.

Passing on a family business to the next generation has not been widely successful over the years. According to the National Centre for Family Business in Dublin, only about 13 per cent of family businesses manage to survive until the third generation and around three per cent to the fourth generation. Sometimes the family business survives but the business family does not.

In this chapter, I discuss the transitioning of the management of the business to the next generation, rather than the ownership.

We saw earlier that few family businesses have a formal succession plan in place, and this affects the chances of the next generation succeeding. There are two sides to transitioning the business to the next generation: the plan and structure decided upon by the business and the preparedness of the next generation.

The next generation member must ask themselves, 'Do I want to join the family business?' and 'Why?'

Too often, there is either an expectation that the next generation are to join the business or it is just assumed without any detailed or meaningful discussion.

Many family businesses are built around the skills of the founder, who had the natural entrepreneurial skills to start and grow a business. To survive and prosper, the family business needs fresh infusions of entrepreneurial drive and passion to adapt to changing market conditions. What many families don't realise in time is that this entrepreneurial drive might not come from family members but from non-family on the management team. There is nothing wrong with that. Often the next generation are not 'entrepreneurial' in the true sense but are good custodians of the business and can bring it on to the next stage by employing the right skills.

Founders can get very frustrated at the lack of entrepreneurial skills in their children. Sometimes the next generation grow the business through acquisition, and many have been successful with this strategy. However, without the proper governance structures in place, it is not uncommon for the next generation to make disastrous acquisitions and risk the future of the family business as a result. Ideally, you want the next generation to try different ideas and be allowed to fail, but the risk must be measured. It shouldn't be allowed to bankrupt the company.

To illustrate some of the pitfalls that can face a family business being passed on between generations, let's take a look at the Bronfman family and what became of Seagram – the world's largest producer and distributor of distilled spirits (until things went wrong).

The Bronfman family emigrated from Moldova, where they were prosperous tobacco farmers, and settled in Canada. The family first got involved in running hotel bars. There were four brothers and their business skills varied. Harry, the second born, emerged as the leader of the family firm – however, he was arrested and accused of bribery. Despite his being acquitted, the family scandal caused a rift between the brothers. Allan, the youngest, went on to qualify as a lawyer and joined the business, but was sidelined by the third oldest brother, Sam.

In 1922, Sam, known as Mr Sam, got control of running the business and never looked back. The banning of alcohol sales in the United States under the Volstead Act provided Sam Bronfman with the opportunity to expand his spirits business in Canada, keeping the market supplied. They took Johnnie Walker into their stable and then acquired Seagram Distillers, a struggling Canadian distilling business. By the end of Prohibition, Seagram's was North America's leading distilling business. Mr Sam commissioned the Seagram Building in New York.

Sam had four children. The two daughters were never considered for business. He had a son, Edgar, in 1929, followed by Charles two years later. Both sons joined the business, with Charles taking a more passive role than Edgar, who was much more ambitious; Edgar tried to build his power base but was constantly thwarted by his father, who never retired and died aged 82.

Sam did not let Edgar have much if any decision-making power and Edgar and his father were in constant battle. When Sam died, Edgar couldn't wait to get going on reshaping the business. In 1981, he sold the stake in Texas Pacific which his father had acquired for €2.1 billion, which was many times the price that had been paid for the stock. The board wanted Edgar to use the funds to build up the consumer goods side of the business, but Edgar wanted a purely financial investment. He acquired 20 per cent in Conoco Oil and a similar stake in DuPont chemicals. He now ran a hybrid between an investment company and a consumer goods company. His 20 per cent of DuPont was worth €308 million and by the time he 'retired' it was worth €8 billion.

Edgar had become an internationally renowned figure and in 1981 he became leader of the World Jewish Congress.

In 1986, without any warning or consultation with his younger brother Charles, Edgar announced that he was appointing his second son Edgar Jr to be the successor in the firm. Edgar Jr had fancied showbusiness more than the family firm. (In 1992, he produced the unsuccessful movie *The Border*, starring Jack Nicholson, and he also wrote the lyrics for the Celine Dion hit 'To Love You More'). However, despite his lack of commercial experience, he formally took over the very large and successful organisation in 1994. His appointment was not opposed by the board of directors, nor his brother or his uncle Charles.

By 1995, the stake in DuPont was 70 per cent of Seagram's total earnings and Edgar Jr wanted to sell it to get into the entertainment business. With the proceeds of the €9 billion sale, he followed his dream and bought Polygram from Philips for €10.4 billion, then 80 per cent of MCA for €5.7 billion, plus Universal Pictures.

Recorded music sales had reached their peak in 1999. It was an industry already under threat from the Internet. In the next decade, streaming became the dominant method to listen to music.

In 2000, Edgar Jr led Seagram into an all-stock acquisition by French conglomerate Vivendi. He traded the family control block of Seagram (24.6 per cent) for more than 8.6 per cent of Vivendi. Edgar Jr became chief of the new company; Vivendi and Seagram effectively lost control of their entertainment business. The beverage side was acquired by Pernod Ricard and Diageo and divided up between the two firms. Seagram, for all intents and purposes, ceased to exist. Vivendi piled up large debts and the share price collapsed. By 2002, Edgar Jr was gone from Vivendi Universal.

Unperturbed by the decline in recorded music sales, Edgar Jr acquired the Warner Music Group in 2004 for €2.6 billion from Time Warner and served as chairman and CEO of the music company for the following seven years. The company went public in 2005 with share values around €30 per share. More than half of its music sales were now coming from digital products.

This case study serves to highlight many issues relating to family businesses, and how not to do things: the lack of a family business charter, weak governance and a weak board, poor succession planning and the destruction of a family legacy. The unmaking of the family dynasty was not so much about the money lost, estimated to be around €3 billion, but the lack of controls in a family business and how such sheer bad judgement was allowed. Sam Bronfman ruled with an iron fist and gave his son no room to develop the business. Edgar Sr overcompensated and gave his son Edgar Jr a free rein. It is a classic case of 'Shirtsleeves to shirtsleeves in three generations'.

Although most of the Bronfman family and their descendants are extremely wealthy individuals, there is no Seagram's business left to pass on to the fourth generation.

Preparing the next generation

To be successful, there needs to be more of a plan than simply letting all the next generation work in the business from an early age. If, after much discussion, the next generation want to join the family business, then you need to put in place a career plan for each member. This should start as early as possible. Children need to understand how money is earned, saved and invested. They need to understand the value of money and that it does not just come out of the ATM of Mum and Dad. They need to understand how the business got to be where it is today and the sacrifices made. You might even advise on the subjects they pick for their school examinations.

Their choice of university and their choice of course should also be examined in light of their desire to join the family business one day. The course does not need to be 100 per cent relevant to the business but it helps if it is. In many countries, the younger generation study business and entrepreneurship as they relate to family business. Amazingly, there is often a shortage of next-generation members who qualify as accountants or lawyers, two very useful professions to have in a family business. While at university, they might get to meet other next-generation family members of their own age and begin to discuss some of the challenges and complexities of running a family business.

Wealth guilt – or, conversely, arrogance – is often a factor in next-generation behaviour. These younger family members may be very good academically but their wealth – which may be disproportionate to their school friends' – can alienate them, or they may find that they attract 'friends' due to their wealth.

While the family member is in college, however, they should be invited to attend a few meetings of the business to get a feel for the issues of the day.

In the family rule book, it should state that the family member must work for a minimum of three to five years in a management position in a company unrelated to the family business. Nowadays, many family members also choose to work in a different country to gain experience.

Family members should join the business in a designated job. Ideally, they will be replacing someone that left or doing similar work to someone else. They should not join as Vice President of Sustainability if no such position exists, or if they have no experience.

Family members should also be interviewed for the job in the business. They should prepare just as if they were applying for a job in a business to which they have no connection. They should be interviewed by non-family executives and have an honest review done of their interview. This rarely happens and it is to the detriment of the family business and the individual.

The family member should be assigned a mentor and this person should feel free to give advice, support and encouragement.

The next generation should also join groups such as Family Business Network (FBN), which operates in most countries. Networking with your peers and people in similar circumstances as family business members will be invaluable.

There are a number of excellent courses run by family business centres attached to the main business schools of the world that are well worth attending.

Many universities do excellent research in the area of family business – covering succession planning, next-generation transition, etc. – but it is very difficult to access. Unlocking this vast source of information to make it available to family businesses is something the universities must do. The academic staff must adapt this research from being written for an academic journal such as *Family Business Review* and write it in a user-friendly version for businesspeople.

If a family member is anxious to progress within the business, the same process should be in place. They should apply for a vacancy, be interviewed and appointed.

When they move up the ladder to be considered for a senior role such as managing director, the board should appoint an interview panel and the family member be interviewed alongside non-family executives, and the best fit appointed.

Coping with different visions and priorities

As I have mentioned before, the sustainability agenda is deeply embedded in the thinking of the next generation. They want to embark on the sustainability journey by focusing on environmental, social and corporate governance (ESG) and social justice. The previous generation probably focused on economic principles and a sense of family values. The current and future generations will want to see societal and environmental values added into the business's core values while continuing to generate economic outcomes. The older generation will be asking to see the returns from a sustainable business model.

Many conversations between the generations need to take place. For a family business to develop a sustainability programme, family members must not let emotions ruin communication. The next generation need to demonstrate new opportunities, innovations and cost savings to show new competitive advantages for the family business. They may have new ideas on strategic partnerships outside of the company which may not have been considered previously.

Covid-19 was a challenge, but it gave the family a lot more time to chat. We all agreed that what we are doing should be meaningful. Not just for the wellbeing of the business and family but for the broader communities where we live and work. I agreed with this as long as it didn't affect profitability and if it did, it should make us more profitable!

TIP

Constant dialogue and discussion between family generations are essential to aligning different vision and values. The next generation should keep in mind that 'patience is a virtue' and the incumbent generation must not block out the next generation until they get frustrated and conflict arises.

Potential problems

Family members need to be kept motivated. People are living longer and working longer, and this goes for the family generation in situ. It is not unreasonable to expect family members to be running the business into their seventies if they choose to do so. This would mean, however, that the next generation are then adults and still not in charge. It can be difficult to keep family members motivated for that long. Frustration can increase on the part of sons and daughters who may well feel they should be in charge and are struggling to establish credibility, particularly with their spouse and children. Of course, sometimes the son or daughter is just not up to the task, and this too causes tension. The parent running the business can see the flaws, but the other parent can only think of 'fairness'.

Many children might realise that they struggle with the challenges associated with running a family business themselves but are too afraid to admit it for fear of being a disappointment or for fear of diminished status outside of the business.

If a business is doing well, family members will already be benefiting from the wealth created by the business, and they may have become accustomed to a lifestyle of privilege. This carries risks, the biggest being the possibility of losing their desire to work.

Conclusion

The potential for conflict and upset for parents and children is enormous; many families have been ruined by the strains of trying to work together. This is especially true for succession planning, which can be a particularly sensitive issue. Throughout this book, the recurring theme is communication. Honest and open communication is essential for navigating these issues. Empathy between parents and offspring comes from good communication. This can be difficult, and the use of non-family facilitators is to be encouraged. Don't put pressure on family members to join the business if they don't want to and equally don't let them join the business if they are not up to the task. Let them know they can opt for a Plan B.

8

Money & Wealth

I made a lot of money as the company grew and prospered. I didn't stop to think how this new-found wealth would affect the rest of the family. My children enjoyed the privileges and opportunities wealth has given them, but they felt isolated from their friends in school who had less money. There was a certain amount of 'Keeping up with the Joneses', unintentionally. We should have talked more about the effect money and wealth had on the family.

Money is probably one of the main sources of conflict and emotional turbulence in family life. We have all heard the saying 'Money does not bring happiness'. Wealth does, however, bring power, privileges and influence. Families of 'old money' learn to live with it but sudden or rapid wealth can cause all sorts of behavioural and psychological problems.

There are three stages of financial success: creation, management and transition. In the life cycle of a family business, the first generation, for example, are busy building the business. They may start to enjoy the fruits of the labour, move to a bigger house, get nice cars, go on nice holidays. The children are carried along on the varying stages of a more affluent lifestyle. These changes in lifestyle can be confusing for children and, as their families become wealthier, it can be difficult to adjust psychologically. They keep seeing their lifestyle change. Also, their school friends may not have any such lifestyle change and the wealth can be isolating.

It can be difficult for family members that inherit wealth and who do not realise how hard it was to create it in the first place. It is particularly difficult for children of the second and third generations. They are the silver spoon generations. They know no different. People tend to mix socially in their income/social class. It can be hard to motivate yourself if you have a lot of money. You don't need to be in the super-rich category like the 7th Duke of Westminster, who inherited £9.3 billion at the age of 25, for it to be a problem. How do you teach children with a lot of money the value of it? It is not easy. Having a lot of money handed to you does affect your motivation to earn your own money. People with a lot of money are also prone to attracting 'hangers-on' who are around them for the lifestyle rather than genuine friendship. Money also brings temptations and access to a lifestyle of partying, drinking, drugs and so on. It is difficult for children to find their own net worth. Old money families can be better at educating their children on how to handle wealth, but not always.

Wealth also puts tremendous pressure on the next generation in family businesses. They don't want to fail.

They don't want to be the weak link in the chain when the family history is written. They are generally very well educated – however, they are sometimes removed from the real world and making money does not come naturally to them. Relationships become transactional. They can become disenfranchised. When they join the family business, they either try too hard to show their usefulness or they do very little in the way of wealth creation.

Warren Buffett said that he wanted his children to have 'enough money so that they would feel they could do anything, but not so much that they could do nothing'. It is a very difficult balance to strike. Some rich family business owners decide to leave their children very little and give away most of their money to charity. Although this is relative – how much is very little? Bill Gates plans to leave each of his children €10m. This is small in relation to his overall wealth but certainly not to the average person. Anita Roddick of The Body Shop, in contrast, gave away all her wealth.

TIP

Talk about money and wealth with your children. Discuss their money and wealth from an early age. Money should not be a taboo subject. No matter how wealthy you are, try and encourage your children to earn money independently, outside of the family business, through school and college. The link between money, value creation and success is a key conversation family business members must understand. The ruination of the current generation entering the family business is not having earned any money independently and living for too long on the bank of Mum and Dad.

Many family business owners do not think early enough about how to manage wealth and separate family wealth from business wealth. Managing wealth should be intrinsically linked to the culture, values and vision of the family.

Once these conversations are had, they form the basis for wealth management, which is a dynamic process and will change over time. For example, in the life cycle of the family business, as the company is growing from start-up stage there is little thought given to the separation of family wealth from business wealth. Any money earned is ploughed back into the business. It is only when the family business is up and running and in the growth phase that there needs to be some separation of thought on family wealth versus business wealth, and advice sought on how to make this happen.

Get professional advice

The market is full of wealth advisors and tax experts. It is important to add these to your team of advisors as the company creates wealth, but be careful of the tendency to have fragmented and uncoordinated or conflicting advice. Too many advisors will run up high fees.

There may come a stage where you should consider opening a 'family office' to manage the family wealth. Some family businesses confuse this with their bookkeeping and accounting function for the family, but the family office is much more – it is a private family company that analyses your wealth and how well you are maximising its use. It plans a portfolio approach to your assets and advises on potential investments.

As the next generation join a family business, set in place a measurement system to identify the wealth created in the years ahead. Why so many family businesses fail by the third generation is that they had everything handed to them on a silver spoon. They often had no ability to create wealth and in many cases were far too good at spending money.

9
Exit Strategy

I had never considered selling the business as an option until I got an offer out of the blue. I was full of mixed emotions that clouded my thinking. I felt disloyal to the business I founded and disloyal to the family but then my family business advisor put me straight – the offer was too good to turn down.

If a family business is trading well and has built up a good market share and reputation, it is inevitable that approaches will be made to sell the business. Far too often, the family business owners are not properly prepared to analyse such an approach and have not thought this through as an option.

The founders of many of today's tech businesses started a business with an intention to sell it or merge it in some form within a relatively short period of inception, definitely within a decade of starting the business.

In more traditional industries, however, such as farming and retail, there is a sense of legacy that features strongly in the equation. There is a desire to hand over the family business to the next generation and this desire very often is the reason to reject any offer for the business.

Sometimes the decision should be fairly straightforward. For example, if there is no suitable family member capable of taking over the business or no family member is willing to do so, then one option could be to sell the business. Of course, there is another option, and this is to hire in or appoint a non-family member to run the business and the family retains ownership.

Alongside the conversations regarding succession planning, there should be one about the option to exit the business if that makes sense both commercially and for family reasons. Again, it goes back to the motivation to sell:

- **You may just want to retire.**

- **You may have decided that there is no family member suitable to run the business.**

- **There may be no clear succession plan and a solution cannot be found or agreed to by the next generation as to how to run the business in future.**

- **Running the business is causing strife and tension in the family and selling the business is the chosen route to maintain or salvage family harmony.**

Other factors to consider

If you ask any family business, they will tell you about the offers they have had for the business. At the peak of the market and the economy, family businesses have turned down generous offers only to find that when the market hits a low, the offers are now a small percentage of those made at the peak. That's life, but it can be frustrating if you didn't sell because you thought you owed it to the next generation to keep the business for them and they have not delivered.

If you look at the history of success in selling a family business and exiting, you will see that the best time to sell is when a business doesn't have to, and it is trading at its peak.

Sometime the current generation leave it too late to consider selling the business and all their money is tied up in it, or the business evolved in such a way that it would not stand up to proper due diligence if there was a buyer hovering.

TIP

You should manage your business as if it were a public company, with the proper structure and proper governance. If a surprise offer came about, your company would be able to show that it has been appropriately managed with the proper controls in place, accounts up to date and good business planning, and you would be able to demonstrate the growth prospects for the business. You must be in a position to sell even if you choose not to.

Unfortunately, it is more common than not to hear of family businesses that decide to sell, and probably have gone through a lot of painful discussions to get to this stage, only to find that the business fails to attract a buyer.

Putting your family business on the market is difficult and not something that comes naturally. To successfully sell your business you need to employ the right advisors with the right connections. Families selling a business often tell after the event how emotionally draining the process was and how much time was put into the sale that left them drained.

Timing is also extremely important. Maybe the timing is brought about because of circumstances relating to the family. It is important that it is right from a market perspective too.

Does it matter who you sell your business to?

Family businesses can be reluctant to sell to their main competitor. The rivalry over the years can be similar to that experienced in sport. It is quite emotional. Leaving aside the emotion, the best price can very often be achieved by selling to a competitor as they will gain market share and economies of scale by acquiring a competitor. Again, you will need good advice from a team of advisors – financial and legal – to help you navigate through the process of selling. It is critically important that you don't disclose confidential information about your business until you are sure that the potential buyer is serious and that you have the right non-disclosure agreements in place.

It is always a good idea to build the company's profile and to increase the company's PR in advance of putting the company on the market. This is not just about increasing brand awareness but tailoring a message about how well the company is doing and maybe hinting at an acquisition to put companies off the scent that your real intention is to sell.

TIP
It is always a good idea to talk to families that have sold their businesses and to ask them why they sold and what process they went through. You will learn a lot from this. You'd be surprised to hear all the different factors that came into play before a final sale took place.

From an early stage, the family business must decide whether it sees itself as a legacy business to be kept for future generations. The most typical quote in these circumstances is 'I'm merely the custodian of the business for future generations'. Other families will have rules around a potential sale in their constitutions. The apt quote for these family businesses is 'Everything is for sale, if the price is right'.

10
Communication

The overriding theme of this book is that communication between family members is crucial to success. Many of the potential conflict situations I have outlined could be avoided by better communication. Good communication is so fundamental to being both an effective family and an effective business, but is extremely difficult and does not come naturally. To run a successful family business, you must have effective family communication as well as effective business communication. Good communication means that information and feelings are conveyed clearly and constructively and received and understood successfully.

All families are unique. Some are loud and boisterous, with everyone fighting to get a word in edgeways, while others are more reserved. Every family has its own way of communicating and that style is an integral part of building healthy relationships.

Conformity and communication are linked in family businesses. Conformity in beliefs, attitudes, values and behaviour can strengthen a family but only if they can get to that point through discussion. It often depends on the style of the parents – traditionally the father – who probably set up or run the family business. Parents can foster warm conforming behaviour where they communicate their ideas in a way that is not dictatorial in terms of hierarchy and instead promotes warmth and closeness.

One scenario might be an autocratic one where the founder demands a high level of conformity in the family which in style can lead to low levels of conversation. Sometimes a family can have low conformity, which might lead to high conversation levels but there may be no unity. The amount, breadth and depth of conversation between family members varies from family to family. It can also depend on family size. It may be difficult to be heard in a big family. Understanding how families communicate is so important is because families bring their style of communicating into the workplace when running a family business. This may not always be conducive to best practice in business communication.

Communication takes patience and an ability to stand in the other person's shoes. I find this much harder to do than running the business.

What is effective family communication?

Communication within families is often very direct. People use a tone of voice, tell other family members what to do, and family members react in forms of learned behaviour. This can be effective but not necessarily easy to understand if you are not family. Families learn ways to be heard and have their views known, but they can also develop bad habits such as interrupting or talking over each other or finishing each other's sentences.

In the family situation, communication must take account of the different roles – parents and children – and their views that come with the different stages in life. A great way to foster communication is to use role-playing: have parents and children reverse roles and continue the conversation. Allowing family members to express their feelings is essential. It will not only reduce stress and anxiety but make them better communicators. However, many families don't know how to control yelling and arguing, which is really detrimental to effective communication. If people are allowed to speak their minds without getting shot down, this will develop a bond between family members and create an environment of trust. Effective family communication creates an environment where family members are comfortable sharing their thoughts, feelings and opinions.

> **TIP**
> Take the time as a family to chat and really understand what is going on in everyone's lives. Family holidays and events are great conversation points. Positive communication helps to build trust and trust is essential if you are going to work together.

Remember, a method of communication that works for families might not suit the business environment.

In business, effective communication means allowing everyone to freely share their thoughts and views, being open to new ideas and listening to differing points of view. We must take the time to stand in the other person's shoes and consider their position. This requires sharing and openness, and the conversations can get quite emotional. It may surprise you to hear that poor communication is very common in family businesses: it plagues them. It leads to lack of professionalism, confusion, conflict, mistrust and a general dysfunctional environment. Contrary to most people's idea of working in a family business, communication can be very informal, haphazard and confusing. Communication in a family business must be even stronger than in a non-family business environment for these reasons.

Communication must be open and honest for all – family and non-family. Meaningful communication should create conflict and differences of opinion. This is healthy but there can't be different agendas. Information should be shared openly. There should be no hidden agendas. Issues need to be addressed head on, whether they be about remuneration, job functions, reporting, poor performance, getting rid of dead wood or succession. Clear and honest communication is often avoided as family members have memories of bad experiences when they talked honestly, so they stay quiet to avoid conflict. This is no way to run a business.

The strength of a family business is the sense of shared purpose. This can get blurred as more and more family members join the business. It is essential to draw up detailed written plans for the business that help members concentrate on strategy and away from personalities.

It may also be very useful to engage an outside facilitator to chair discussions and put some order into proceedings.

In our business meetings, the family members all speak over each other, finish each other's sentences, repeat themselves and stray off the subject constantly. This is the way they must talk over Sunday lunch, but it causes havoc in the office.

Often conversations within families follow a set pattern, which may have been set from the time you were young; one family member, for example, may dominate conversations. A common scenario might be that the person running the family business is busy, comes home exhausted and tries to catch up on what has been happening in the family in their absence. Sometimes they are greeted with a barrage of questions and demands and often retort with the familiar, 'Ask your mother/father.' Or one parent wants to make a point but feels they won't be able to enforce it, and says, 'Your father/mother will be very angry when he/she finds out.' No one gets any real training to be a parent. Both parents have come together from two separate and different families and bring with them the way they were taught to act in their respective families.

Every family member has a unique communication style, a way in which they interact and exchange information with others. You need to understand the patterns of communication for each family member and how this communication flows. Communication within a family is extremely important because it enables members to express their needs, wants and concerns to each other. Strong families are often said to stick together but truly strong ones communicate well together. Understanding each other is key to bonding. Families are there to help and protect each other and this sense of loyalty is one of the key strengths of families.

> ## TIP
>
> Pick the right time and place to have discussions. Choose the right medium. Certain topics might be best introduced over the phone, maybe even by text message for the younger generation but probably not by email! You can't beat face to face if it is important. Put proper thought into how to structure the conversation – should it happen in the office or at home? Does it involve multiple family members? Should it be formal or informal?

Many of us think we are good communicators. In reality, I don't think many are as good as we like to think. Some of us are good talkers (essential for selling), but so too is listening. We are not good at listening. We think we are being clear and precise, only to find out that we are misunderstood. It's more complex in family businesses. Families often develop their own unique styles of communication. Body language is intuitive and a very important part when we are speaking together; outsiders find it hard to understand what is going on.

Remember, communication is a two-way process. Open, honest and clear communication should be the overriding principle. Lack of time and being busy is always used as the excuse for poor communication. Make time in everyone's busy schedule to stop and talk.

Make sure you don't conflate the roles – a parent may also

be the CEO; they may wear two hats, and likewise for all the family. Make sure the way you communicate fits the role you are playing. Try and distinguish between facts and feelings. Family members often assume they know how another member of the family will feel or think on an issue. Be a good listener and try not to bring bad communication practices from the family environment into the business setting.

Some families have a culture of little or no conversation. Some have a culture of lots of conversations, often being capable of discussing a topic freely and openly. Some discussions end up with a parent making the final decision, not heeding the discussion that took place. Some families make collective decisions. Others have a more laissez-faire approach and give their children certain freedoms to make decisions. Some family members do not trust certain others to make the right decision, so they make it for them.

Storytelling is a vital part of communication for a family too. Think of tribes and how they pass on traditions to the next generations. It is through storytelling. Parents telling stories to their children about what they experienced growing up gives the child a sense of values and belonging. All tribal stories help the family function as a cooperative unit. Telling a story is a way to communicate a lot of information in a memorable way. For tens of thousands of years, stories have served to pass down lessons in how to live from one generation to another.

Storytelling is also vital for family businesses. It is extremely important to tell the story of the family business not just to the next generation but to all stakeholders. Family businesses can learn from other family business stories.

Information processing is a vital component in the

successful running of a business. A lot of information in a family business, especially in first-generation businesses, is passed informally and sometimes it gets to some people and not others. Keeping things simple beats being complicated, but without structure, some people are still on plan A, not realising that others have moved on to Plan B.

To lead a family business, you must be good at communicating the vision and goals of the business. Good communication is a core characteristic of a good business leader. Don't assume everyone knows. Tell them, discuss with them, listen to them and be open to feedback and criticism.

Write decisions and plans down, especially the important ones. Very often family business meetings are held, a discussion ensues and decisions of sorts are made. Unless these decisions are captured and written down, they can be communicated differently by different members that were present in the room, causing confusion.

TIP

Effective communication takes a lot of time and effort to get it right. Stop and re-examine how you are communicating as a family and then re-examine how this is being brought into the business. If you are not communicating properly as a family, you will not communicate properly in the family business.

11

The Future for Family Businesses

Family enterprises have been with us since the start of mankind. Despite enormous changes in the way business is conducted, family businesses are still the cornerstone of commerce today, but will this always be the case?

The future is not so clear. As I have indicated, massive changes are happening with families. Families are changing, getting smaller, becoming less cohesive and more complex. Greater opportunities to do other things, greater mobility and greater choice may affect the desire to join the family business.

The future for family businesses will vary across the world. In the developing world, family businesses have a bright future for many years to come as traditional industries with cheaper labour tend to thrive in this part of the world.

Traditional industries such as farming, hospitality, construction and services will eventually all be affected in some way by automation and technology. Families must develop their businesses into a world of new opportunities such as increased online business in the wake of Covid-19.

Family businesses tend to be in it for the long term. In contrast, the entrepreneurs starting up technology companies these days do not generally hire family members and are conditioned to flip their businesses within a fairly short time span and diversify their wealth.

The recent Covid crisis has shown us that resilience is one of the key factors behind successful family businesses. Family businesses have been key to the survival of many economies. They have become stronger. The more cohesive and aligned family businesses took decisive action under pressure, which in turn provided a sense of security and stability to their workforce, customers and other stakeholders. Most family businesses came up with creative solutions to keep as many staff employed during Covid, sometimes even foregoing family salaries to keep employees on the books.

Family businesses recognised that many of their customers were in difficulties also. Supply chain uncertainties added to the difficulties but good communications with customers helped them work together to find solutions. The ability to move fast and make decisions quickly and their overall agility set family businesses apart. While big corporations were having multiple Zoom meetings discussing 'pivoting', family businesses were already pivoting instinctively without ever using buzzwords.

The time has come for governments and financial institutions to recognise family businesses as unique and distinctive drivers of the economies of the world. Specific policies should be put in place to support family enterprises. They are a force for good in all economies.

They support their communities; they retain their employees longer in downturns and the majority of good ones adapt quickly and maintain their long-term focus.

It has been my pleasure and privilege to have worked with great family businesses all over the world. The experience has been truly inspiring.

I hope you have enjoyed reading this book and that it's provided some thought and discussion for your family, your employees and your business.

Families are complex, full of no-go areas, full of inherent conflicts, full of sorrow and joy. We didn't get to choose the family we ended up in. It can be near impossible to get on with everyone all of the time, but the enjoyment comes from belonging. The clever ones work hard at being a functioning family. When a family is operating as a unit, blood is definitely thicker than water.

Business is complex, and the odds are stacked against running a long-term, successful business.

Add family and business together and you get a near-impossible task. If you navigate through the choppy waters, the fruits of your labour will be immense. Clear and honest communication is the bedrock.

If you are in a family business, and you can navigate the rigours of business and the dynamics of family life, you are on the road to being the next Walmart (Walton family), Bacardi, Bose, Sun Hung Kai Properties (Kwok family), Dyson, Reliance (Ambani family), ALDI (Albrecht & Heister families), IKEA (Kamprad family), Kohler, Mars or JCB (Bamford family), to name a few. Good luck!